BABY STEPS

MILLIONAIRES

—

No discipline seems pleasant at the time, but painful.
Later on, however, it produces a harvest of righteousness and
peace for those who have been trained by it.
—Hebrews 12:11 NIV

BABY STEPS

MILLIONAIRES

How Ordinary People Built Extraordinary
Wealth—and How You Can Too

DAVE RAMSEY

RAMSEY
PRESS

This publication is designed to provide accurate and authoritative information with regard to the subject matter covered. It is sold with the understanding that the publisher is not engaged in rendering financial, accounting, or other professional advice. If financial advice or other expert assistance is required, the services of a competent professional should be sought.

Scripture quotations marked (NIV) are taken from the Holy Bible, New International Version®, NIV®. Copyright © 1973, 1978, 1984, 2011 by Biblica, Inc.™ Used by permission of Zondervan. All rights reserved worldwide. www.zondervan.com. The "NIV" and "New International Version" are trademarks registered in the United States Patent and Trademark Office by Biblica, Inc.™

Scripture quotations marked (NKJV) are taken from the New King James Version®. Copyright © 1982 by Thomas Nelson. Used by permission. All rights reserved.

Scripture quotations marked (ESV) are taken from The Holy Bible, English Standard Version® (ESV®). Copyright © 2001 by Crossway, a publishing ministry of Good News Publishers. All rights reserved.

Editor: Rachel Knapp
Cover Design: Chris Carrico
Photography: Seth Farmer
Interior Design: PerfecType, Nashville, TN

ISBN: 978-1-942121-59-6

Printed in the United States of America
21 22 23 24 25 WRZ 5 4 3 2 1

This book is dedicated to those who are Baby Step Millionaires
and those who are to come. Your diligence and success are often unassuming,
but your example shouts HOPE and POSSIBILITY to the world
and proves that ingenuity and hard work pay off.

CONTENTS

ACKNOWLEDGMENTS

It's been eight years since I wrote my last book. In that time, our team has grown, gotten more agile, and published another handful of #1 national bestsellers. Even so, I will never take for granted that our books don't *just happen* without the hard work and support of some incredible people. An extra special thanks goes to . . .

Sharon Ramsey, for your unwavering commitment at the top and the bottom of our first million and your constant support since. It's been fun to stand together all these years and see so many others baby step their way to their first million.

Preston Cannon, for your leadership, guidance, and humor through every phase of this fast-paced project.

Jackie Quinn, Michelle Grooms, Rick Prall, Rachel Knapp, and Jennifer Day, for your commitment to excellent content and your outstanding research, developmental, and editorial support.

Tim Smith and the research team at Ramsey, for your diligent work to conduct *The National Study of Millionaires* and collect the stats and stories that powerfully normalize the concept of the Everyday Millionaire.

Chris Carrico, Seth Farmer, and Brad Dennison, for your creative genius on the cover design. You sure do know how to make an old, bald guy look good! More importantly, you've given this thing a chance to get into more hands and change more lives.

Amy McCollom and Michelle Dixon, for your impeccable project planning on our tightest timeline yet.

Caitlin Radecki, Jasmine Cannady, and Russ Sellars, for your marketing and sales know-how and your hearts to serve our readers.

ACKNOWLEDGMENTS

Megan McConnell and the Ramsey publicity team, for expertly spreading this world-changing message far and wide.

Suzanne Simms, Jen Sievertsen, Luke LeFevre, Jeremy Breland, and Brian Williams, for your excellence in leadership and vision and your faithfulness in prayer.

CHAPTER 1

Can Anyone Become a Millionaire?

The rain ran down the kitchen window as Tiffany stood at the stove, boiling water to make what had become her regular, twice-a-day meal—ramen noodles. It was all she could afford. As a twenty-seven-year-old, Tiffany was recently divorced and figuring out how to be a single mom. She felt overwhelmed and afraid—and completely confused about what to do next. She was working more than sixty hours a week but still struggling to support herself and her two babies on a $30,000 a year salary. Plus, she had a staggering amount of debt payments going out every month. She was hanging on by a thread until she decided enough was enough.

Tiffany had always believed God had a purpose and plan for her. But because her life was so chaotic, she couldn't figure out what that plan was or how to get it together. So she started researching ways to get out of debt and build wealth and found the Ramsey Baby Steps.

At first, Tiffany tried to do the plan "Baby Steps-ish"—doing some of it the way it's taught by us at Ramsey Solutions and some of it the way she preferred. But she soon realized that to make progress as fast as she could, she needed to go all in. She couldn't count on child support, and she didn't have anything of value to sell to speed up the process, but she worked extra hours, made tons of sacrifices, and finally saved up enough for her emergency fund. Slowly but surely, she clawed her way out of $60,000 of debt. And with no debt payments, her income was hers to invest. As a young, single mom, Tiffany felt freer and stronger than ever!

Over the next twenty years, lots of life happened. Tiffany unexpectedly lost her dad in a tragic accident, and she battled and beat breast cancer. But she was determined not to let any hardship knock her off her plan. She kept scratching and clawing. She got promotion after promotion at work. Finally, she grew her net worth to $1.85 million! Her diligence resulted in:

- $1.3 million in investments and cash
- $450,000 in real estate
- $100,000 in other assets.

Today, Tiffany is a millionaire—a Baby Steps Millionaire!

Tiffany's now remarried and has become a Ramsey Financial Coach and *Financial Peace University* Coordinator. Her passion is teaching the Baby Steps to others so she can spread the hope and freedom she's come to know in her life. Tiffany is not just a Baby Steps Millionaire. *She's a hero!*

John and Maddi's Story

When John and Maddi married, they brought together a blended family of five kids and soon had a child of their own. But one thing they didn't bring together was their finances, and John had no idea how much Maddi struggled with money.

Maddi's prior marriage had been abusive and controlling. When she was angry, stressed, or in an argument with John, she would self-medicate by going on spending sprees—huge spending sprees, mostly on credit cards. As a result, she racked up thousands of dollars of debt until it all finally came to a head . . .

John pulled his credit report one day and found that he had $20,000 of credit card debt. When John confronted Maddi, she admitted that she had secretly opened several credit cards in his name. John felt heartbroken and betrayed, and after a few years and a lot of tears and hard conversations, John filed for divorce.

Thankfully, their story doesn't end there. After their first mandatory appointment at an attorney's office, John and Maddi left the building at the same time out of opposite doors. But they ended up running into each other on the stairs outside. When they saw each other, it was a turning point. John and Maddi knew they loved each other and realized divorce was the last thing they wanted.

Not long after, a friend invited Maddi to a *Total Money Makeover* live event where I shared the Ramsey Baby Steps. She didn't know who I was and didn't really want to go, but she came anyway. Sitting in her seat that day, she came to a hard but powerful realization—money wasn't the problem. The problem for Maddi was the person in the mirror. Something clicked for her, and she left the event knowing she had to change. And for the first time in a long time, Maddi had hope that she and John could come together on their finances and make their marriage work.

John and Maddi read *The Total Money Makeover* and attended a *Financial Peace University* class at their church. That's when they discovered they were buried in over $300,000 of debt. It was overwhelming, but they now had a plan to attack it—with a vengeance. Through it all, John and Maddi's marriage was transformed. He saw Maddi change her mindset and come alive. She was energized and committed to getting rid of all of their debt as fast as possible.

They put their heads down, sold everything that wasn't nailed down, and adjusted their lifestyle drastically. In just over five years, they paid it all off, including their house! In fact, they were so heads-down on paying off their mortgage that they didn't realize how much their investments had grown in the meantime. When they finally looked up, they weren't just debt-free. They discovered that they were straight-up millionaires! John and Maddi had grown their net worth to just over $2 million. Here's how it broke down:

- $1.5 million in investment accounts
- $475,000 in a paid-for home
- $50,000 in liquid assets.

But even more importantly, John and Maddi worked together and now have a restored and thriving marriage. They even came to Ramsey Solutions' headquarters to do their Debt-Free Scream. I loved meeting them and hearing their story. And you know how they did it? By working together, taking action, and following the Baby Steps. Wow! *John and Maddi are heroes!*

What's interesting about Tiffany's story, John and Maddi's story, and millions of stories just like theirs is that they started from nothing and did nothing fancy. They just followed a plan—the Ramsey Baby Steps—stayed the course, and became millionaires. At Ramsey Solutions, we call them Baby Steps Millionaires—a special group of Everyday Millionaires, people just like you, who used the Baby Steps to reach the millionaire mark. And what you should take from their stories and this entire book is . . . ***YOU CAN DO THIS TOO!***

Now, I get it. As you read this, I can almost hear the voice of doubt in your head . . . *Sure, that's great for Tiffany, John, and Maddi, but there's no way I can do that. My situation is different. I don't have the right degree, I don't have a high-paying salary, I don't come from the right family or neighborhood, I don't (fill in the blank) . . .*

I'm going to let you in on a little secret: those voices aren't doubt! Those are lies from a toxic money culture. Lies told to you by credit card companies, big banks, mortgage lenders, payday lenders—any entity whose business plan includes making a profit by selling you debt and brainwashing you into believing you can't get ahead, you'll always have payments, and you're stuck living paycheck to paycheck.

It's also family, friends, neighbors, admissions counselors, business and government leaders, talking heads in the media—anyone who tells you the only way to become wealthy is to inherit it, be a person of privilege, or graduate from a prestigious school. It's today's toxic money culture telling you all of this crap. But it simply isn't true. Millions have experienced significant life-change because of the Baby Steps, and that means only one thing . . . ***YOU CAN DO THIS TOO!***

Best Practices

In a free society where we're allowed to make our own legal and moral choices, we really can control a lot more of the outcome than we think. Best practices help us do that. Best practices exist all around us in every subject imaginable. In business, when you want to imitate systems that produce optimal results, you study and apply best practices. So, for example, if you want your accounting system to operate properly, you need to learn the best practices used by successful businesses. You don't have to invent accounting. You're not unique when it comes to accounting. And you won't do well looking for shortcuts. There are already tried-and-true accounting processes and principles that work every time. You can try to be special, to be the exception, but you will be wrong, and you'll just make it harder on yourself.

The shortest way to get from where you are now to success is by submitting yourself to the best practices of the thing you want to learn and do well. If you want to be a better parent, study parenting, apply what you learn, and get better. You can also observe great parents who raised children to be successful adults, determine what they did, and copy it. The same can be said for marriage, weight loss, training for a marathon, building a career, constructing a house, running a business, and yes, even building wealth.

When it comes to building wealth, everyone wants the highest probability of success combined with the fastest turnaround time. That's what the Baby Steps are: the fastest method to get out of debt and build wealth, no matter your financial scenario. The Baby Steps are proven. They work every time. There's no situation too unique or too difficult for the Baby Steps. Of course, there are always problems and barriers to overcome. The road to becoming a Baby Steps Millionaire is definitely not a straight line—but the outcome is *not* random.

You reap what you sow. When you plant corn following the processes and principles of successful corn farmers, you WILL grow corn. When you follow the Baby Steps like so many successful millionaires have, you WILL build wealth too.

Tested and Proven

This is a book thirty years in the making. Not because I'm some hero, but because I'm the guy who did stupid with lots of zeros on the end. I made my first million in my twenties—the wrong way—and then went bankrupt. But from there, I learned God's ways of handling money. And from that came the Baby Steps. Using these steps, I was able to become a millionaire again—this time the right way. Since then, my "been there" has allowed me to "be there" for others, to guide them on their money journeys and recover from—or avoid altogether—the same mistakes I made.

For the last thirty years, I've gotten to guide heroes like Tiffany, John, and Maddi as they took control of their money, saved, invested, and built wealth, and more importantly, built the life they'd always dreamed of. *They're the heroes!* They've worked hard to work the plan. I'm just the guide with a plan that actually works.

My goal with this book is to let you in on what I already know—the Baby Steps work, and they can work for you too! *You* can build wealth and become a millionaire—no matter what the culture says, what your barriers are, or what your starting point is. In *Baby Steps Millionaires*, I'll show you how to do it and then walk you through some of the things I've learned the hard way, so you won't have to. These are things you'll face on your journey to building wealth—because part of learning best practices is discovering what obstacles you're up against and how to overcome them.

As we dig in, I'll tell you true stories of real Baby Steps Millionaires. These stories are aspirational and anecdotal. They're not statistically significant in mathematical terms, but storytelling is a valid way to prove truth and show you this is really possible. You'll be inspired by these people—because they're just like you!

I'm also going to share with you the Ramsey Solutions' *National Study of Millionaires.* (You'll find the white paper of the study at the back of this book.) This study was conducted by professional researchers using rigorous research techniques and is the largest study of millionaires ever done in North America. Our research team conducted detailed interviews, surveys, and analysis of over ten thousand millionaires. The conclusions from the data are statistically overwhelming and only confirm what the stories show. You'll see and believe that not only is it possible for you to be a millionaire, but the Baby Steps plan is the fastest way to do it!

Listen, I'm not Superman. I suck at a lot of things—too many to count. I've only become "America's Trusted Voice on Money" because I've shown a lot of people how to build wealth and then *they* did the work. I'm just a guide—someone who's been there and wants you to do better than I did.

The Ramsey Show has been on the air for thirty years and gives me the opportunity to guide over twenty million people every week who are listening by radio and podcast or watching on YouTube. Our *Financial Peace University* class (now a part of our Ramsey+ membership) has taught almost ten million people how to handle money God's way. We've sold over twenty million books, including over eight million copies of *The Total Money Makeover* alone. It blows my mind to think about it! The men and women these numbers represent indicate that the Baby Steps have helped more people get out of debt and build wealth than anything else in America today.

And if millions have experienced life-change over the last thirty years because they've taken the best practices—the Baby Steps—we've developed and successfully applied them to their own lives, why couldn't millions more? Why couldn't you?

That's what this book is about: helping more people like you become wealthy so they can live their dreams and give outrageously. It's a book about hope. A book about belief. A book full of success stories about people like Tiffany, John, and Maddi. And it's also a book about statistical proof. A book about steps to taking action and building wealth. This is not a book that tells the secrets of the rich. It's not even full of sophisticated, hard-to-grasp concepts reserved only for the elite. As a matter of fact, this information is straightforward, really practical, and maybe a little boring. But let me tell you something: the life you'll lead if you follow the best practices I give you in this book will be anything but boring!

Are you ready to do this? It's game on!

CHAPTER 2

What Is a Baby Steps Millionaire?

I first met Webster over fifteen years ago. In a single minute, he permanently changed our guest policies for the radio show. In those days, we actually let fans sit *in* the studio while I was doing live talk radio. Looking back, it seems crazy, but we did it. Let's put it this way: sometimes I'm so friendly, I'm stupid. Webster had been through *Financial Peace University* and was (and still is) a devoted follower of our teachings about money. He wrote and asked to visit the studio when he was in Nashville, and of course, we agreed because we always did.

About six feet away from the broadcast desk and up against the glass were two simple, straight-back chairs that our "studio audience" could sit in. At commercial breaks over the three-hour show, I made many new and lifetime friends with the people sitting in those chairs. Webster and I were on our way toward another one of those friendships when it happened.

Apparently, he had not been feeling well and was maybe a little nervous sitting in the studio because, in the middle of a live segment, he vomited all over the floor. I was trying to keep talking so our listeners wouldn't notice, and at the same time, hand him a trash can to limit the damage. Needless to say, at the commercial break, the whole team hit the studio like a NASCAR pit crew and had it cleaned up before we went into the next segment. Poor Webster had just become a legend. And that was the last day anyone sat inside the studio while I did a live show. Guests now watch from the lobby through a vomit-proof wall of glass.

Webster's story went into the file of really weird and wacky things that have happened in my thirty years of doing talk radio. A few years later, he showed up again and made the story even more extraordinary. This time he came to do his Debt-Free Scream on the show. That's a thing we do—our way of recognizing heroes who've completed Baby Step 2 and paid off all their debt except for their mortgage. Webster reached this milestone and reminded us that he was the guy in the legendary vomit event.

And then, several more years later, Webster added another layer of extraordinary to the story. My old friend showed up again—this time to be on our Everyday Millionaire Theme Hour. This is also a thing we do. It's an hour of the show dedicated to talking with ordinary people, like Webster, who've become millionaires or more. During the segment, I ask them about their habits and what they did to build their wealth.

On this trip to the show, Webster shared that he was now sixty-four years old, and he and his wife had a net worth of $1.45 million. They broke it down like this:

- $1 million was in retirement
- $250,000 in a paid-for home
- $200,000 cash they had recently inherited and put in investments.

These numbers are awesome! But do you want to know what was most extraordinary about Webster's story? He had become a millionaire from nothing. Zero. He was just an ordinary guy living an ordinary life.

Both of Webster's parents had grown up dirt poor in small-town Tennessee. His dad served in the Air Force for twenty years, and his mom had a decent job. They were hardworking folks but spent everything they made living paycheck to paycheck—so that's how Webster learned to live. He became a spender too. If he had $50, he spent $100. His mentality was, "If I want it, I'll buy it."

On top of that, Webster struggled academically. He graduated from high school, but between 1975 and 1987, he made five failed attempts to attend college. It wasn't until 2019 that he discovered he'd been battling a learning disability called dysgraphia, a neurological disorder that impairs a person's writing ability and fine motor skills. It interferes with all practical aspects of the writing process, including spelling, legibility, word spacing and sizing, and expression. But thankfully, dysgraphia didn't keep Webster from doing what he was made to do.

While he was working the night shift as a dishwasher at a hotel, his manager discovered that Webster was good with numbers and technology, so he moved him into an auditor role. Webster took to computers, and with diligence and time, he was able to acquire enough certifications in Information Technology (IT) to make a living at it.

In 1999, Webster started listening to the early versions of *The Ramsey Show*. He'd been married for fifteen years at this point and had grown his income to $36,000 in IT. But even then, he and his wife were on the brink of bankruptcy and divorce. In a last-ditch effort to make things work, they went through *Financial Peace University* and learned about the Baby Steps. Now they had the tools they needed to begin bailing water from their sinking ship.

By 2001, they got hyper-focused—or as we call it at Ramsey Solutions, *gazelle intense*—and took full control of their financial situation. At the time, they were making a household income of $48,000 a year and staring down the barrel of $197,000 of debt. But they got after it, pinched every penny, sold tons of stuff, and paid it all off in only four and a half years! And that's when the real fun began—the wealth-building journey from debt-free to Baby Steps Millionaire.

No longer broke and chained by debt, Webster started seriously investing his way to a net worth of $1.45 million. Part of that process was investing in himself. Being in IT and struggling with dysgraphia, he knew he had to be a continuous learner, so he added IT certificate upon certificate to his resume and continued to grow his greatest wealth-building tool—his income. It paid off! Today he's got a couple hundred IT certifications and makes $180,000 per year. Not bad for a guy who didn't go to college and started in IT in 1977 making $400 per month!

Webster started with nothing, overcame tremendous obstacles, worked on himself, grew his income, and became a legend. My friend Webster is a hero. I am so proud to know men and women like him all over America. He stayed with it and got a little better every day, every week, every year. He is a Baby Steps Millionaire.

What a Millionaire Is and Isn't

Before we discuss how to become a Baby Steps Millionaire, we need to tackle the definition of *millionaire* first. What exactly is a millionaire? And if that's the goal, how do we know when we've reached it? There are lots of misconceptions and illusions out there surrounding what a millionaire is. So, let's cut through the crap together, shall we?

A millionaire is someone with a ***net worth of $1 million*** or more. It is NOT anything else. THAT is the only definition. It's a math formula. It's not a feeling. It's not more than that or less than that—it's simply a math formula. *Net worth* is simply *assets minus liabilities*. It's what you *own* minus what you *owe*.

This definition of millionaire is not a political statement, not a theological discussion, not your feelings or emotions, not the amount of money you make, and not your mother's opinion. (Can you tell I've heard all kinds of absurd arguments over the years?) It's a math formula. If someone has an income of one million dollars or more, that does NOT make them a millionaire. *Net worth* is the only true definition of being a millionaire.

Now, you may or may not have *millionaire* as a goal, but that does not change what makes a millionaire. You may think rich people are all evil or they're all virtuous. In either case, you'd be wrong. There are examples of both, but *millionaire* is not a moral construct—it's a math formula. We'll discuss character and the morality of wealth later, but to confuse those with the actual definition of millionaire would be a false premise and must be set aside before we set out to make YOU a Baby Steps Millionaire.

Some folks say, "A million dollars isn't what it used to be." Correct. But you are still a millionaire. Other folks say, "A million dollars is not enough." That may or may not be correct as well, but if you have it, you're still a millionaire. By the way, having a million dollars is more than most people who are whining about these things have.

Let's look at Webster again. He and his wife have zero debt of any kind, with assets of $1 million in retirement, $250,000 in their home, and $200,000 in other investment accounts, totaling a *net worth* of $1.45 million. That's how you calculate if someone is or isn't a millionaire. There is no other formula. We'll discuss later what it means to live like a millionaire, but that doesn't change the formula either.

One of the statistics we discovered in the Ramsey Solutions' *National Study of Millionaires* is that the average time it takes someone to become a millionaire is seventeen years . . . We're talking, *Ready, set, go!* But what was the typical starting point? For the ten thousand millionaires we surveyed, it was the point in time when the person woke up and realized they *could* become wealthy and *could* set out on a sacrificial plan to get there. They may have been coasting along, investing and living frugally, but then they became very intensely goal-focused. Or when they decided to change, they could have been (and usually were) in debt with no plan at all, but then got sick and tired of being sick and tired. In Webster's case, he started his get-out-of-debt journey in 2001, and it took him four and a half years. Then in 2005, he was debt-free and began to seriously build wealth. Sixteen years later he was on my show as a Baby Steps Millionaire!

Baby Steps Millionaire Defined

In Chapter 1, I defined *Baby Steps Millionaires* as a special group of Everyday Millionaires who used the Baby Steps to reach the millionaire mark. An Everyday Millionaire is someone who became a millionaire starting from nothing without inheriting any money.

I introduced the 7 Baby Steps in my first *New York Times* bestseller, *Financial Peace*. It was self-published in 1992. Then Viking Press published it, and it hit the *New York Times* list in February of 1996. In 2003, the Baby Steps on steroids and every detail on how to walk this clear path to wealth was compiled into a book called *The Total Money Makeover,* which has now sold over eight million copies and logged over one thousand weeks on the bestseller lists. I share these dates and numbers only to show that for a LONG time a LOT of people have used and are using the Baby Steps to not only get out of debt but also become wealthy—to become Baby Steps Millionaires.

The Baby Steps are a simple, clear plan designed to help you best manage your money and build wealth. They are seven specific steps given in a determined order so you know what to make your first goal, second goal, and so on. The Baby Steps give you the shortest, surest path (notice I didn't say the get-rich-quick path) to becoming a millionaire. You work the plan steadily, taking one small bite at a time, reaching one goal at a time, until one day you're a Baby Steps Millionaire.

As I mentioned, the Baby Steps are covered in detail in *The Total Money Makeover*, but for those of you who are new to the plan, or who need a review, let's do a quick drive-by.

Baby Step 1

The first Baby Step is to save $1,000 for your starter emergency fund. The goal is to save it as fast as you can. Your emergency fund will cover those unexpected life events you can't plan for—because Murphy will come knocking. Murphy's Law guarantees that if anything can go wrong, it will go wrong. In other words, if you're alive, bad stuff will happen to you sooner or later. It's not even about being pessimistic or negative—it's just a fact. Sooner or later, it's going to rain, and that's why you need an umbrella.

For example, you might have an experience like a woman on our team who had her $1,000 saved and was on Baby Step 2, working hard to pay off her debt. Out of nowhere, her tooth split from top to bottom. It was extremely painful, and she had to have it extracted. Murphy didn't care. It just happened, and so did the ridiculously high dental bill to go with it. The whole fiasco wiped out every penny of her emergency fund, but because she had it, the money was there to use. Even though it didn't cover the entire bill, that $1,000 turned what could have been a crisis into an inconvenience and made it much easier for her to cash flow the rest of the balance. And the best part was, she didn't have to go deeper in debt to pay for it!

Having $1,000 set aside will safeguard you from digging a deeper hole while you're trying to work your way out of debt. And that brings us to Baby Step 2.

Baby Step 2

Baby Step 2 is to pay off all debt, except the house, using the debt snowball. If you have any money above your $1,000 emergency fund that is not in a retirement plan, cash it out, and use it on Baby Step 2. Also, temporarily stop all investing to free up all cash to hit Baby Step 2 with a vengeance. You're going to put yourself on a scorched-earth, no-room-for-fun budget and pay off your debt like your life depends on it. Great gazelle intensity and focus for a short sprint are what's needed here. You do this by using the debt snowball method.

If you're reading this and thinking it's impossible, search our show archives for some truly inspiring Debt-Free Screams. Those stories will make you a believer! Your most powerful wealth-building tool is your income. When you quit giving your income away to credit card companies, student loans, and car payments, you'll have the money to invest and become a Baby Steps Millionaire!

Baby Step 3

The third Baby Step is to save three to six months of expenses in a fully funded emergency fund. A proper rainy-day fund is three to six months of bare-bones living expenses that can *only* be used for an emergency. Now that you have no payments but a house payment or rent, you have tons of room in your budget. So quickly beef up that starter emergency fund of $1,000 to a fully funded emergency fund. This will protect you against life's bigger surprises—like a medical emergency, job loss, or your car breaking down—without slipping back into debt.

If you're wondering what amount is best for you to save, ask yourself: *Is my household income stable?* If so, then saving three months of expenses is probably enough. If you're a one-income family, self-employed, on straight commission, or have a special circumstance like a medical condition that requires frequent doctor visits, then saving six months of expenses is the best choice. Remember, this is about feeling prepared to cover your bare minimum expenses if a big emergency strikes. This is not about maintaining your current lifestyle and still affording concert tickets or dinner out.

These first three steps take the average Baby Stepper in *Financial Peace University* about two and a half to three years to complete. The same is true for *The Total Money Makeover* reader. That's the average. It takes some people a shorter amount of time and some people a longer amount of time. Remember, Webster took four and a half years. Getting rid of non-mortgage debt and having the fully funded emergency fund allows you to really pump up your investing and not destroy your progress with every emergency that comes along.

These first three Baby Steps are foundational to protecting and growing your wealth. The plan is simple, but it's not always easy. You'll have to deal with the person in the mirror. There will be days when you want to quit. You'll miss going to restaurants and working out at your fancy gym. Your beater of a car may break down—more than once! You'll be disappointed when you have to cut your beach vacation from the budget. Your family and friends will laugh at you and think you're crazy for following the Baby Steps. But winning at anything requires sacrifice. Hebrews 12 says that no discipline seems pleasant at the time, but it yields a harvest of righteousness. That means if you will live like no one else now, later you can live and give like no one else.

The first three Baby Steps must be done precisely in order. As tough and rewarding as they are, this book is not about the first three steps. This book is about how wealthy you can become *after* you save for emergencies and get out of debt. I want you to get out of debt *so that* you can increase your generosity, become wealthy, and ultimately, change your family tree. So, how do you do that? Let's move on and take a look at Baby Steps 4–7. This is where it starts to get really good—where your millionaire journey begins.

CHAPTER 3

—————

How to Become a Baby Steps Millionaire

Usain Bolt is an eleven-time world champion sprinter, popularly known as the fastest man alive. At the Berlin 2009 IAAF World Championships in Athletics, Bolt set a world record time of 9.58 seconds for the 100-meter race, with an average speed of 23.5 mph. Between meters 60 and 80, he clocked 27.8 miles per hour![1] That's just stupid fast! I feel like throwing up just thinking about a human being running at that speed.

On the other hand, you don't need to be able to pronounce his name to know Eliud Kipchoge is renowned throughout the world as a marathon poster boy. He's an eight-time major marathon winner and four-time Olympic medalist. He set the world record in Berlin in September 2018, clocking an official time of 2:01:39. A year later, he did what no one thought possible. He broke the two-hour barrier, finishing an unofficial marathon in Vienna at 1:59:40 with an average mile pace under 4:34 minutes.[2] Wow! That's just crazy fast!

Both Kipchoge and Bolt are elite runners. They both have God-sized ability, remarkable genetics, and the mental toughness to train at extreme levels and win. However, because of the specific strategy each has taken to prepare for their particular type of running, they couldn't easily swap races and be successful. Sprinters train for agility, stamina, and explosive power. Their weight training is focused to build power and speed, and they are visibly more muscular than marathoners. Marathon runners are more physically lean and train to build endurance for long distances. They work to develop their mental strength just as much—if not more—than their physical strength.

The Baby Steps involve both types of strategies, but working the plan is not an elite sport. And the great news is, you don't have to be Bolt or Kipchoge to win. Anyone can reach the finish line—even bald guys built more for bowling than running! Think of Baby Steps 1–3 as the 100-meter dash—a relatively short, intense burst in the scheme of the whole race route. It requires putting on your sprint spikes and going all out for an average of two and a half to three years. It takes agility and explosive power to break through mountains of debt and build up emergency savings.

Baby Steps 4–7 are the longer leg of the race and require a completely different strategy. In these later Baby Steps, *you're changing your intensity to intentionality.* You're lacing up your marathon shoes and mentally preparing to endure the long run over about seventeen years. Sprinters don't stop for nutrition or water. They power through with all their mind, body, and spirit to the finish line. Marathon runners stop for nutrition and water along the race route, and they develop a slower and steadier rhythm that allows them to spread their energy over a longer run.

During Baby Steps 4–7, you can go out to eat again, buy a couch, go on vacation, save to buy a home (if you don't own one), and budget for enjoyment and entertainment. (Of course, you no longer borrow money, so you're budgeting all these things as cash purchases.) Intentionality simply means you're now doing money on purpose. You happen to money; it doesn't happen to you. Simple math tells us that the more you consume in Baby Steps 4–7, the slower your wealth progress is, so you will need to strike a balance. If there's no fun, you'll flame out. If there's too much fun, you'll never arrive at Baby Step 7, the final step. Let's look in a little more detail at the last four steps. (Again, if you want all the details, you can check out *The Total Money Makeover.*)

Baby Step 4

This is where the magic starts to happen. In Baby Step 4, you invest 15% of your pre-tax household income into retirement investments. Here's how to decide where you should put the 15%:

Multiply your whole gross household income by 0.15 to know the amount you should be putting in all combined accounts. The most mathematically efficient placement of the money is a little like Rock-Paper-Scissors, but it works only one direction: Match beats Roth beats Traditional, like so:

1. First, take all the company match you can get—100% return on investment trumps everything else.

2. Second, do all the Roth you can at work or as an individual. In most retirement accounts, over 90% of the balance is growth at retirement age, and no taxes on that growth means hundreds of thousands of dollars gained.

3. Next, after you have filled the two buckets above, and if you still haven't allocated the 15% of your income, then put the rest in a traditional tax-deferred plan through your work.

Again, Match beats Roth beats Traditional. (Side note: Even though an employer match on any part of your investment is nice to have, don't count it toward your goal of investing 15% of your gross income. Think of it more like icing on the cake of your own contributions.)

Baby Steps Millionaires invest like I do—in good growth stock mutual funds with long track records. I evenly invest my personal retirement in four types of funds:

- **25% in Growth and Income**
  These funds create a stable foundation for your portfolio. They're basically big, boring American companies that have been around for a long time and offer goods and services people use regardless of the economy. You'll want to be sure to look for funds with a history of stable growth that also pay dividends. They

might be listed under the *large-cap* or *large value* fund category. They may also be called *blue chip*, *dividend income*, or *equity income* funds.

- **25% in Growth**

  This category features medium or large U.S. companies that are experiencing growth. Unlike growth and income funds, these are more likely to ebb and flow with the economy. For instance, you might find the company that makes the latest "it" gadget or luxury item in your growth fund mix. Common labels for this category include *mid-cap*, *equity*, or *growth* funds.

- **25% in Aggressive Growth**

  Think of this category as the wild child of your portfolio. When these funds are up, they're *up*. And when they're down, they're *down*. Aggressive growth funds usually invest in smaller companies. But size isn't the only consideration. Geography can also play a role. Aggressive growth could sometimes mean large companies that are based in emerging markets.

- **25% in International**

  International funds are great because they spread your risk beyond U.S. soil and invest in big non-U.S. companies. You may see these referred to as *foreign* or *overseas* funds. Just don't get them confused with *world* or *global* funds, which group U.S. and foreign stocks together.

These are solid long-term investments. Notice there aren't any short-term investments in my portfolio. The internet is full of people with opinions about investing. The number of broke people writing money blogs while living in their parents' basement boggles the mind. You can choose what you want to do. This is a book about what I've done and what millions of people have done to become wealthy. If you don't want to do this plan, that's fine—do yours. But *this* is the plan the Baby Steps Millionaires have done to build wealth.

Investment Returns

Since 1928, the S&P 500 (the benchmark of American stock market performance) has averaged an 11.46% rate of return.[3] There is a lot—too much—discussion out there about the rate of return you can expect. The weird thing is that it doesn't matter much. Our study of millionaires and our interaction with Baby Steps Millionaires reveal they weren't the best investors on the planet. They didn't spend hour upon hour deciphering long academic formulas to get the best returns. The typical millionaire is, at best, an average investor.

Their secret sauce to building wealth? *They actually invest*; they don't just talk about it! And they never stop investing. They keep going and going and going and going. They don't time the market, jumping in and out based on some guru.

Research by the American Academy of Actuaries, aka accounting super nerds, says that 80% is a "useful measure" of savings rate for retirement investment success, but maintaining 100% savings rate is the healthiest retirement strategy.[4] *Savings rate* is how much you save and how often you do it. In other words, 80–100% of your success in investing is based on the fact that you actually DO IT. Rates of return, asset allocation, and expense ratios on the investments only account for 20% or less of your success. Translation: *Actually investing every month, every year, every decade is substantially more important than all your other investment analysis.* So, stop arguing with your broke brother-in-law about investment theory and just freaking DO IT.

Investment Professionals

Now that you're investing, let's address some other things I personally do and have recommended to Baby Steps Millionaires for thirty years. When picking mutual funds, it's best to have an investment advisor in your corner to teach you. They must have the heart of a teacher because you must learn, not simply follow, their suggestions. You want them to be able to explain complex concepts in ways you can understand, but not tell you to do something with a "because I said so" attitude and a commission-hungry spirit. At Ramsey Solutions, we're not in the investment business, but I use and recommend people in the business to advise me and you. We call these people SmartVestor Pros.

Using a SmartVestor Pro for our company 401(k) and my personal Roth IRAs, I've been able to outperform the market over thirty years using the four fund types. John Bogle, the founder of The Vanguard Group and creator of the first index fund, said that "mutual funds can make no claim to superiority over the market averages."[5] So, his point was that you might as well just buy index funds and forget it. Since 80–100% of winning is simply investing, then he is actually correct. You can become a millionaire following his advice.

However, I am a glass-half-full guy. If I have a tee time at 9:00 am and there's a 62% chance of rain, that tells me there's a 38% chance of sunshine—so I'll be at the golf course to play. In the same way, if even 70% of mutual funds don't outperform the market, that means I should be able to find one of the 30% of funds that DOES outperform the market.

Keep in mind, though, that the few points I beat the market by is *not* the secret sauce. *Actually investing* is the most important part. Sixty-eight percent of Everyday Millionaires in Ramsey's *National Study of Millionaires* said they use an investment adviser to give them input and guidance but not make their decisions.

Basic Math

Not only can you become a Baby Steps Millionaire following the Baby Steps, but if you actually follow the steps exactly, it's hard to mess it up. Let's look at some math.

Pretend Joe and Suzy are thirty-two years old. They realize they need to make some big changes, and it takes them the average of three years to do Baby Steps 1–3—get out of non-mortgage debt and build their emergency fund. At thirty-five years old, they start Baby Step 4 and invest 15% of pre-tax household income into retirement investments. According to the U.S. Census, the average household income today is $65,712.[6] So to keep it simple, let's say Joe and Suzy make a household income of $65,000. Following Baby Step 4, they would invest 15% of their $65,000 income into good growth stock mutual funds. Fifteen percent of $65,000 is $9,750 per year or just over $800 per month. Now, let's pretend they don't get *any* employer matching (which is unlikely because a majority of employers do match), and they work their *whole* lives making the average income and *never* get a raise. Crazy thought, right?

My personal mutual funds selected with a SmartVestor Pro have averaged over 12% per year. That's more than the stock market has averaged. But even at 10 and 11%, an

$800 a month investment over thirty years will put Joe and Suzy well above the million-dollar mark:

- $800 per month from ages 35–65 at 10% return is $1.8 Million
- $800 per month from ages 35–65 at 11% return is $2.2 Million
- $800 per month from ages 35–65 at 12% return is $2.8 Million

So even if you want to argue about rates of return or expense ratios or whatever else, you must admit that even if I am *half* wrong on my assumptions (I'm not), you will *still* become a Baby Steps Millionaire. Of course, Joe and Suzy's income will go up! And of course, no one's life ever happens in a straight line! And of course, life never happens exactly according to basic assumptions!

What happens out here in the real world as opposed to a blogger's theoretical world is that when Joe and Suzy get out of debt, start actively and wisely managing their money, and invest steadily, they will prosper inordinately. Their marriage will be more likely to last. Their careers will explode because they'll be free to make choices. Their generosity will go way up. And all of this ensures that they will actually become crazy wealthy.

Remember Webster? He started his whole money journey beginning the Baby Steps at age forty-four and investing for only sixteen years—not thirty years—and he still became a Baby Steps Millionaire! So, what if your income was $80,000 and you were the same age as Joe and Suzy? At 10% growth you would have $2.2 million, not $1.8 million. And if your income was $100,000, you would have $2.8 million.

To further expand on the crazy world of math assumptions, here's an easy calculation for you to use. If your investments are averaging 10%, a lump sum with no additional investing will double about every seven years. So, if due to employer matches and increased income, Joe and Suzy hit a $1 million net worth fifteen years in at age fifty and STOPPED investing, this is what it could look like:

- At age 57 they'd hit $2 million
- At age 64 they'd hit $4 million
- At age 71 they'd hit $8 million.

That is with only fifteen years of investing and never saving another dollar! The bottom line is this: if anyone tells you that you can't become a Baby Steps Millionaire, it shows their ignorance of basic math.

Now, I'm not saying that once you get to this point in the Baby Steps it's all unicorns and rainbows. Some people make it through Baby Steps 4–6 quickly. For a lot of people though, the struggle and discipline of living out these later steps is very real. Just because it's the marathon portion of the race and your pace is slower than a sprint doesn't mean it won't still suck at times. You're no longer chained by debt, but it's a long-distance run. And marathon runners know all too well the grueling symptoms of fatigue, leg cramps, and nausea that can affect the time it takes to finish the race.

You might have to drive an older, beat-up car longer than you thought you would. Your monthly budget might still be tight while you're giving away 10%, investing 15%, and cash flowing a modest vacation. And Murphy doesn't magically disappear once your emergency fund is fully funded. It can be rougher than you think to be on these later Baby Steps and have to completely deplete your emergency fund because Murphy staged a sit-in. A friend of mine experienced this. He and his wife had to replace two new HVAC units, a roof, and a car transmission all at once. Ouch. It nearly wiped out their emergency fund. He told me he was glad they could cash flow those expenses, but it *really hurt* to write those checks.

This is the reality of the Baby Steps. The money is there for an emergency—that's the point—but you're also used to it being there on an emotional level. That safety net has given you a sense of security, and when it's gone, it's painful. If your emergency fund gets wiped out, you have to pause Baby Steps 4–6 and go back to Baby Step 3 to rebuild your emergency fund (yes, that means pausing your retirement contributions for now). Going back a step can feel like you're losing ground, but you have to keep in mind that this is the purpose the Baby Steps serve. They give you the sequence for how to navigate the unexpected. It may suck for a while, but it's temporary—and you'll rebound faster than you think.

As frustrating as it can be, there's no quick-fix, snap-your-fingers way to build wealth and avoid Murphy. But here's what you need to remember: sticking to the Baby Steps, avoiding debt at all costs, and paying cash for things you need and want is still the fastest way to become a millionaire.

Baby Step 5

Baby Step 5 is saving for your children's college fund. Now, it's important to note that, while Baby Steps 1–3 happen in strict order, Baby Steps 4–6 happen simultaneously. For thirty years, we've seen these three steps work best in tandem because it's the *fastest* way to build wealth. So, if Baby Step 5 applies to you and you're already investing 15% into retirement, you should also, at the same time, fund your children's college fund through a 529 college savings plan or an ESA (Education Savings Account).

This step is intentionally vague because the amount you need or want to put into your children's college fund will vary from zero to a lot. You may not have kids, you may have grown kids, or maybe you don't plan to pay for college. On the other end of the spectrum, you may have a fifteen- and seventeen-year-old who want to go to college, but you have little money saved. That means you'll have to get creative and lean in hard.

The reality is, you might not be able to scrape up enough for college when the time comes. If you can't, you're not alone. There are lots of wonderful, loving parents who simply can't afford to put their kids through college. There's absolutely no reason to feel guilty about this. *And* you should *not* sacrifice your retirement savings to do so. Paying for college is a nice thing to do, but it's not a moral obligation. Plus, there are all kinds of options out there for your kids to get an affordable higher education.

Here's the deal, and it might sting a little: there's no guarantee that your kids will even *go* to college. And if they do go, there's really no guarantee they will *graduate*. But there's a 100% chance that you'll retire. At some point, your body will tell you it's time to stop punching the clock. If you don't take care of your retirement savings, you'll be left to count on Social Security. (Or should I say, social *insecurity*?)

The main thing to remember about college is, whether you're paying for it or your kids are: do it with NO DEBT. Your kids can go to a more affordable school, get scholarships, and work to pay for it as they go. In our #1 bestseller *Debt-Free Degree*, we outline in detail how a debt-free degree can happen in *any* scenario. It's possible, just like becoming a millionaire is possible.

Baby Step 6

In Baby Step 6, you pay off the house early. In our *National Study of Millionaires,* we found that 67% of millionaires have a paid-off home, and it took them an average of 11.2 years to pay it off. Take that in for a moment: Millionaires don't spend thirty years paying off their house. They pay it off in roughly ten years. They're also not living in a 10,000-square-foot mansion. They live, on average, in a 2,600-square-foot home they've been in an average of seventeen years. So, it's clear that this step is about living intentionally. You're not living in your parents' basement but you're also not spending outlandishly. Again, intentional means *on purpose.* When you have money beyond the 15% you're putting into retirement and beyond whatever you're putting toward college, you'll need to throw it at your home mortgage.

As you progress in your career and your income increases, maybe your plan will be to apply your raises toward doubling your mortgage payment every other month. Maybe you have stock options as part of your compensation package or receive stocks as a bonus for a job well done. Then you can do what one couple from Idaho did. They took any and all vested stock the husband received as a bonus for his work as an electrical engineer, and they threw big chunks at their mortgage whenever they could. By doing this, they were able to pay off their mortgage seven years early! When you get intentional and have a plan to attack your mortgage and pay extra whenever and however you can, you'll save tens or even hundreds of thousands of dollars in interest, *and* you'll likely pay off your home in around ten years or less from the time you hit Baby Steps 4–6.

Paying off your house is a very important part of your millionaire equation. We've discovered that the typical Baby Steps Millionaire has two main parts to their net worth as they build their first $1 to $5 million. For the vast majority of people, their wealth break-down looks like this:

- Two-thirds of their net worth is retirement savings
- One-third of their net worth is their paid-off home.

We've seen over and over again someone with a $1.8 million net worth who has a $600,000 paid-for home and $1.2 million in their 401(k) and Roth IRAs. Webster fit this observation fairly closely with $1 million in retirement, $250,000 in their paid-for home, and $200,000 in other investments. Once someone gets beyond $5 million or so, the ratios and investment mix will change. We'll discuss the dynamics of this wealth category later in Chapter 4.

Baby Step 7

The final Baby Step is to build wealth and give. You know what people with no debt can do? Anything they want! So imagine what people with no house payment or debt of any kind *and* a huge dose of intentionality can do. You guessed it! Build wealth rapidly and be outrageously generous.

You can have a monthly giving amount set aside to do spontaneous things, like the couple who left cash and a "Keep Going!" note under the windshield wipers of a beater car. The car had a bumper sticker that read, *Dave Ramsey makes me drive this.* Or you could be ultra-intentional like one couple who paid off their son's and daughter's mortgages! Baby Step 7 allows you the freedom to be intentional with the inheritance and legacy you'll leave to your loved ones someday. And I guarantee that giving outrageously is the most fun you'll have with money!

The point is simple: If you want the shortest possible path to becoming a Baby Steps Millionaire, you need to work Baby Steps 4–6 simultaneously *and* with intentionality. This will cause you to become a millionaire, on average, in seventeen years or less after you hit Baby Step 4 because you'll be able to build wealth in mutual funds and pay off your home in ten or so years. The calculations above and the data points across thousands of millionaires yell loudly, *YOU CAN DO THIS TOO!*

CHAPTER 4

A Millionaire Is Not a Billionaire

Imagine making $152,000 per minute. That's almost $2.3 million in just fifteen minutes! Crazy, right? It's hard to believe anyone could make that kind of money at that rate. But Jeff Bezos, founder and former CEO of Amazon, does.[7] He's what I call *uber wealthy*. What Jeff makes while he's on a coffee break is what the average American worker with a college degree earns over the course of their career. Just think about that!

Bezos is in a completely different category of wealth than the rest of us mortals. He's moved well beyond millionaire status and is even pushing past the limits of billionaire status. In July of 2021, the richest man in the world had a net worth of $211 billion.[8] In technical terms, he's actually considered a centibillionaire. "Centi" represents a unit of one hundred. So, just like "centi" signifies a centipede has one hundred legs, "centi" means Bezos has over $100 billion. That's just ridiculously rich! At the time of this writing, there are only ten people in the world who can claim the status of centibillionaire, with Jeff Bezos, Elon Musk, Bill Gates, Mark Zuckerberg, and Bernard Arnault claiming the top five spots. So, what in the world does that type of billionaire wealth look like?

In addition to Amazon, Bezos has extensive business holdings, including Zappos, Whole Foods, and *The Washington Post*. Bezos has so much money that spending $1.95 million feels the same as the average person in America spending $1. And when Bezos buys a private jet for $65 million, that would be kind of like you spending $35 for a new pair of jeans.[9] See what I mean? Uber wealthy!

Bezos actually owns two Gulfstream private jets worth almost $120 million. These are some of the fastest jets in the world. He also owns a bunch of cars most people can't even pronounce, including a $3 million Ferrari Pininfarina, a $4.8 million Koenigsegg CCXR, and a $5 million Lamborghini Veneno.

Bezos is one of the largest real estate owners in the United States. He built a huge mansion in Beverly Hills, California, for $165 million. This mansion has eight bedrooms, ten bathrooms, and includes an extravagant koi pond, tennis courts, European garden, spa, waterfall, and a courtyard with an outdoor fireplace. This is in addition to another Spanish-style mansion he owns in that area worth $25 million. He also owns a $96 million three-level, 23,000-square-foot penthouse in New York City overlooking Madison Square Park, featuring seven master suites and a 5,000-square-foot rooftop terrace with a pool.

In addition to these mansions, Bezos has a 5.3-acre estate in Medina, Washington ($20 million), a townhouse in Washington, D.C. ($23 million), and three other apartments in New York City ($17 million). And let's not forget the 400,000-acre ranch in Texas that serves as his headquarters for his space transportation program.[10]

While space travel seems extravagant (because it is), that's just the latest aspect of the uber wealthy lifestyle of Jeff Bezos. Bezos's space exploration company, Blue Origin, designed the New Shepard reusable rocket and space craft that provides an eleven-minute space flight. In the summer of 2021, Bezos made huge headlines with the first-ever private space flight. He and his brother, Mark, claimed two of the three seats on the flight, and the third seat was auctioned online to an individual for $28 million.[11] For the math nerds out there like me, that works out to $2.5 million per minute or $42,424 per second.

In addition to his extensive philanthropic giving and support of many causes around the world, Bezos has spent over $42 million since 2018 in an effort to have a 500-foot clock built inside a mountain cave in West Texas. Because, why not? The clock is called the

Clock of the Long Now and is intended to tell time for ten thousand years and chime once every thousand years.[12] (The big question is, who will be around to hear it?)

So much of Bezos's lifestyle is unrelatable and even completely unfathomable. And it should be—because he's a centibillionaire! My point is this: a millionaire is NOT a billionaire.

One of the biggest hurdles people face as they think about building wealth and becoming a millionaire is all the mistaken ideas of what rich people look like. People confuse having a million dollars with living a Bezos kind of life, with big luxury mansions on private islands and a personal yacht and jet to take them there. But we need to get one thing straight: a millionaire does NOT in any way live the same life as the uber wealthy billionaire. This is *so important* to get clear in your head. Being a millionaire is an entirely different thing than being Jeff Bezos. The Baby Steps will make you a millionaire, but they won't make you a billionaire.

No Space for Confusion

A millionaire—a Baby Steps Millionaire—looks something like this . . . At thirty-seven years old, Clint and Brittany have a net worth of $1.3 million dollars. Clint learned about the Baby Steps in his senior year of college. His mom was going through *Financial Peace University* at the time and had given him the CDs to listen to (for you younger readers, that's those round audio discs we once played in a boom box . . . thankfully, the product is all digital now). As soon as he heard the teaching, something clicked for Clint. From that point forward, he started viewing debt as the arch enemy of wealth.

Clint and Brittany quickly started on the Baby Steps. They immediately cut up their "came with a free t-shirt" credit cards they got in college and paid off Clint's $4,000 truck loan. After they graduated, they zeroed in on Clint's $12,000 student loan. They both started out with good jobs in their fields of study (construction management and industrial engineering) making $84,000 combined, but they still made the very intentional choice to get gazelle intense and go into extreme sacrifice mode. The way Clint tells it, they lived off basically nothing and didn't spend money on anything but the cheapest apartment they could find. It worked! In just sixty days, they knocked out the $12,000 loan and never looked back. They stayed laser-focused, finished their fully funded emergency fund, and started investing.

Without leveraging borrowed money or inheriting a single dime, Clint and Brittany followed the Baby Steps and grew their net worth of $1.3 million to look like this:

- $620,000 in 401(k) and Roth IRA accounts
- $380,000 in home equity and real estate
- $300,000 in cash and other savings.

And they did all of this by age thirty-seven! That's impressive! And it falls right in line with how we've seen people over and over complete Baby Steps 4–7 and become a millionaire in seventeen years or less. Remember, that's starting with no inheritance.

Sixteen years after Clint and Brittany graduated college, they've grown their combined income from $84,000 to $225,000 per year and seen their early sacrifices and commitment to following the Baby Steps produce huge dividends. They started from nothing, followed the plan, got out of debt, completely avoided debt, saved and invested, and now they're Baby Steps Millionaires. Clint is currently the vice president of a construction company and Brittany is a quality manager at a carpet manufacturer. They're making over $200,000 per year, don't have a payment in the world, and have $1.3 million at age thirty-seven!

Now compare Clint and Brittany's lifestyle to Bezos's. They own a 2,100-square-foot, three-bedroom, two-bath home that they bought in 2012 and paid off in 2015. Their big "splurge" wasn't space exploration but paying cash for more living space—a six-acre property that they plan to build a 3,600-square-foot custom home on in the next one to two years. They still mow their own lawn and wash their own cars. They own three paid-for vehicles: two 2016 Honda Civics and a 2005 Chevy Colorado. And when making big purchases or planning family vacations or activities, they still look for any coupon code or deal they can find.

When I told Clint that I imagined he would be worth $10–20 million at age sixty-five, he said, "Yes, that would be the goal." Clint and Brittany aren't confused; they know exactly what they want their lifestyle to look like now and in the future. Yet every week I coach people who want to become Baby Steps Millionaires but are blocked by confusing the idea of millionaire with billionaire. Again, it's thinking $1.3 million is a Bezos life. But Clint and Brittany blow this notion out of the water! They've built a solid life from their work in construction and carpet manufacturing that will set them up to retire with dignity and leave a strong financial legacy for their family.

Most people don't grow up wealthy. I didn't grow up wealthy. Clint and Brittany didn't grow up wealthy. And visualizing how something looks, feels, and works is hard for anyone who hasn't seen or experienced it before. That's why it's easy for people like me to make mistakes—even huge mistakes—about something they've never personally done or gone through.

A few years ago, my son and I went to an exotic race car track to rent uber expensive cars and go really fast. Unlike Bezos, I'd never been in a car like a Ferrari or Lamborghini before, much less driven one. And I'd especially never driven anything over 165 mph. As a car guy, I will never be the same. It blew my mind. I had never felt G forces, acceleration, sound, and sensation like that before, so I had no idea how incredible it would be. Watching others drive cars like that in the movies or on the racetrack, I thought I knew what it would be like . . . but my personal experience was way different and way better than my assumptions.

The same is true for mountain climbing. If you've never climbed Mount Everest at 29,032 feet or done the simple 6,643-foot climb to the top of Clingmans Dome in Great Smoky Mountains National Park, then you might think they are the same. They are both mountains. They are both a climb. They both require equipment. When you get to the top of both, you will feel a sense of accomplishment. But they are nowhere near the same.

Nowadays, I own and run a company that has revenues of hundreds of millions of dollars a year. Having started from a card table in my living room, I often find that while I can intellectually grasp our numbers, I've not always kept up emotionally. I can still remember the hopelessness that drove me to sit at that card table in the first place. I had debt leveraged up to my eyeballs and was running like a gerbil on a never-ending wheel of unpayable payments. I can remember me at twenty-eight years old, sobbing in the shower, wondering how my family and I were going to survive bankruptcy. Now, when we spend more on a computer system or software purchase than I used to make in a decade, it's emotionally weird. And I don't ever want to take for granted that I've experienced both scarcity and abundance. Boiled down, both involve money and business. Yet they are two very different experiences.

Millionaire versus Billionaire

Just like my Ford Raptor is not a Ferrari, just like Clingmans Dome is not Mount Everest, and just like my card table thirty years ago is not the Ramsey Solutions of today . . . a Baby Steps Millionaire is NOT a billionaire. A million is 1000 x $1,000. A billion is 1000 x $1 MILLION. A billionaire has a thousand times more wealth than a millionaire. ONE THOUSAND TIMES! So, if you have $10,000, you are ten times closer to being a millionaire than a millionaire is to being a billionaire.

I wrote this book to convince you that the first level of wealth—becoming a millionaire—is attainable and that the process is fairly simple, even boring. In effect, this book is meant to normalize the concept of becoming a millionaire and give you the clear Baby Steps path to get there. It is meant to make you see, feel, and understand that becoming a millionaire is realistic, reasonable, and within your reach. If your goal is to jump straight to billionaire, you should read a different book.

So, what does a millionaire's life generally look like as compared to a billionaire's life? Here are some key distinctions:

TRANSPORTATION

- Millionaires often own two cars, something like a nice Ford pickup and slightly used Mercedes, ranging in the ballpark of $30,000–$50,000 each.

- Millionaires do not own private jets or helicopters.
- Billionaires often own seven to ten cars, something like an Aston Martin, Ferrari, Lamborghini, or a custom-ordered, top-end model of a more common brand, ranging in the ballpark of $150,000–$300,000 each.
- Billionaires often have their own private jets or helicopters.

HOMES

- Millionaires own a paid-for home and maybe a beach condo.
- Millionaires probably live just down the block from you in a normal residential neighborhood.
- Millionaires often still cut their own grass.
- Billionaires own five to seven homes all over the world.
- Billionaires don't even think about cutting their own grass. They have a full support staff of maids, chefs, house managers, etc., to run their private estates, which are protected by the most cutting-edge security systems and fenced off from the nearest neighbor.

BUDGET

- Millionaires still pause when reading the menu at a nice restaurant. They start reading on the right, where the prices are.
- Millionaires use coupons. Ninety-three percent of millionaires in *The National Study of Millionaires* shop with coupon discounts.
- Millionaires carry a list at the grocery store. Eighty-five percent of millionaires in *The National Study of Millionaires* shop with grocery lists.
- Billionaires don't worry about coupons, shopping lists, or the prices on any restaurant menu; they shop and place orders without thinking.

The HOW Is Different

Every year, *Forbes* magazine puts out a list of the four hundred wealthiest people in America called "The Forbes 400." In 2020, the "poorest" on the list had a net worth of $2.1 BILLION, and the average net worth was over $8 billion. That year, Bezos topped the chart at a whopping $179 billion.

It might surprise you to know that 70% of the Forbes 400 are "self-made," meaning their wealth was not inherited. Even Bezos grew Amazon into the e-commerce giant it is today from the humble beginnings of his garage in Seattle.[13] It might also surprise you that 93% of millionaires surveyed in Ramsey's *National Study of Millionaires* are also "self-made" and didn't get wealthy through an inheritance either. But based on what you now know about the Baby Steps, it shouldn't come as a surprise that millionaires use a completely different process than the billionaires on the Forbes list.

As we said in the last chapter, Baby Steps Millionaires all got that way from following the Baby Steps exactly as they're outlined and steadily investing and paying off their homes. That same process will NOT make you a billionaire, ever. That first level of wealth may position you to take the next steps to billionaire, but none of the Forbes 400 simply funded their 401(k).

Most billionaires own their own huge national company and/or took it public and the stock made them wealthy. Some of them sold their large company and that event made them billionaires. For instance, that's how Mark Cuban did it. In 1999, he and his old college friend and business partner Todd Wagner sold their online audio-video streaming company Broadcast.com to Yahoo for $5.7 billion.

Mark grew up in middle-class Pittsburgh, Pennsylvania. His dad worked in a car upholstery shop. To pay his way through college, Mark taught dance lessons. He worked at a bank and also sold computer software after graduating college until his entrepreneurial spirit took over and he started his first company, MicroSolutions. When he sold that company to CompuServe for $6 million, he was still on the millionaire track. It wasn't until his second company, Broadcast.com, went public in 1998 and its stock reached $200 a share that the switch flipped, and he jumped from millionaire to billionaire. Remember, a billion is 1000 x $1 MILLION. So, from one company sale to the next, Mark jumped from $6 million to almost one thousand times that—1000 x $5.7 MILLION! He went from starting an internet streaming company with his college buddy so they could listen to Indiana Hoosiers basketball games online, to now owning the Dallas Mavericks NBA team.[14] Big difference.

Even LeBron James recognizes how big of a difference this is. In the 2021 season, he was expected to make $95.4 million through his on-court contract and endorsements and was projected by Forbes to surpass $1 billion in career earnings.[15] That's a lot of money! And it would make him the fifth active athlete and the first team sport athlete to ever achieve this. But this is just career earnings, not necessarily billion-dollar net worth. Like Cuban, LeBron has aspirations to own an NBA team someday, but on average those run a $2.2 billion price tag.[16] In one purchase, that would take his entire career earnings and then some!

My reason for pointing out the dramatic differences between millionaires and billionaires is simple. If you incorrectly apply billionaire attributes to being a Baby Steps Millionaire, it could make you or others lose hope that it's doable. And it is *very* doable! We're not trying to buy NBA teams here! We're trying to create a life and retirement that's not stressful and choked by debt—one that will meet all your financial needs while allowing you to be generous and create a healthy financial legacy for your kids. But if you're expecting to live like a billionaire when your net worth is like Clint and Brittany's $1.3 million, you will be sorely disappointed. They're nowhere near the same thing. Billionaires are much more rare, and it's a thousand times harder to become a billionaire than a Baby Steps Millionaire—literally.

Mark Cuban's journey to becoming a billionaire might have inspired you to build and sell a high-ticket company one day. That's awesome! Go for it! But if you want to become Mark Cuban, Jeff Bezos, Oprah Winfrey, Sam Walton, Warren Buffet, or any other billionaire, you would use a different process than the Baby Steps. However, if on your way to a billion, you want to have a net worth launching pad of $1 to $10 million, then the formula here is not only doable, it's ridiculously accurate.

Melanie and JD's Story

Baby Steps Millionaires Melanie and JD found it to be an easy formula. When asked which of the Baby Steps was the most difficult, Melanie told me, "I don't think any of them were really difficult for us. We would have gotten there eventually, but the Baby Steps gave us a plan to get there faster."

Melanie first heard about the Baby Steps while listening to *The Ramsey Show* on the radio during one of her many drives to visit her then boyfriend, JD. During their college years, JD lived in South Carolina and Melanie lived in Georgia. She spent many miles driving between the two states, listening to me over the airwaves talk with people and teach them money principles. The more she listened, the more she realized the Baby Steps were principles she and JD already believed in, but it gave them a much clearer plan to follow.

They had both always been natural savers and relatively debt averse. With the help of their parents, co-ops, and internships, they were able to avoid taking on student loans during college. But after college, both she and JD did what they thought every college grad does—get real jobs and buy nice cars with car loans. "They were kind of like our gifts to ourselves for getting real jobs," said Melanie. It took a few years of feeling the pain of those car payments to get fully on board with the Baby Steps, but once they did, they knocked out their loans quickly.

Out from under their debt, Melanie and JD settled into married life and worked to grow in their careers. With JD working as a mechanical engineer in the nuclear field and Melanie working for a civil engineering and architectural company, you would think they were making crazy amounts of money, but they started out making average incomes. JD made $60,000 a year and Melanie made $50,000 a year. Their secret sauce was following the Baby Steps, staying gazelle intense with their savings, and making wealth-building a priority. Even though their friends and family thought they were crazy and couldn't understand why they wouldn't go out to eat or why they would save for things instead of taking out loans, Melanie and JD kept pressing forward.

On long car rides to visit family, Melanie and JD continued to listen to *The Ramsey Show*, specifically tuning in to the Everyday Millionaires Theme Hour. As a young married couple, it became their favorite segment. They would listen and dream about what it would be like to be millionaires someday. They made it a goal to become Baby Steps Millionaires before they were forty years old—and they did it!

Not having debt payments freed up a lot of their income and allowed Melanie and JD to save while still enjoying life. It also allowed them to move through the Baby Steps quickly. They got married in 2013, and by 2018, they were in Baby Step 7 with a paid-for house! Did you catch that? It took them less than five years to completely pay off their house using the Baby Steps! They saved enough to put 50% down and took out a fifteen-year mortgage. Each month they threw as much as they could at their house payment. At the same time, they both maxed out their retirement accounts and started Roth IRAs.

Today, JD is thirty-six and Melanie is thirty-seven. They now have a son, and after reaching a high combined income of $200,000, Melanie was able to pause her career and stay home with him. With lots of focus and determination, JD and Melanie made their dreams come true! Now, instead of hearing stories of how others have met their goals on the Everyday Millionaires Theme Hour, they're living their own Baby Steps Millionaire story.

The Baby Steps helped Melanie and JD accelerate their goal of becoming millionaires before forty and reach a net worth of $1.1 million dollars without receiving any inheritance or leveraging any borrowed money. It breaks down like this:

- $375,000 in a paid-for home
- $575,000 in 401(k)s and Roth IRAs
- $100,000 in savings/investments.

This is what a clear plan plus focused intensity looks like. It's an accurate and doable formula. It's simple and straightforward. It leaves no room for confusion. It's millionaire, not billionaire. It's Clingmans Dome, not Mount Everest.

Mount Everest versus Clingmans Dome

Approximately eight hundred people a year climb Mount Everest. Over eleven million people visited Great Smoky Mountains National Park last year, and over five hundred thousand people made the climb to the top of Clingmans Dome. Two hundred million people did neither. Instead, they sat on their couch, binge-watching Netflix. Everest, Clingmans Dome, and your couch are three very different things.

Climbing Mount Everest

So, what makes Mount Everest so hard to climb?

First, time. You have to travel to the mountain and take a short flight and ten-day trek to Everest Base Camp. And then, you need to stay at base camp for a few weeks to acclimate to the altitude. We're talking months of prep time plus the actual climb—and that doesn't even count the amount of time it takes to prepare your body and mind for a climb like that!

Second, timing. The route to the top of Everest doesn't open until May. And even then, there's only a short climbing window between the harsh, subfreezing winter conditions and the summer monsoons.

Next, conditions. There's an area at around 26,000 feet called the "death zone." Enough said, right? The air is so thin and the conditions so brutal that even with supplemental oxygen, people can experience heart attacks, compromised breathing, and cerebral edema, which causes loss of muscle control, confusion, and hallucinations. Not to mention, climbers can battle frostbite and hypothermia.

Last, resources. It can cost $30,000–$100,000 or more to pay for travel, fees, permits, experienced guides, mountaineering and camping gear, and a week of oxygen and food.[17]

Climbing Clingmans Dome

What does it take to climb Clingmans Dome?

First, time. Clingmans Dome is accessible by car from wherever you are in the United States. Once off the main highway, you can drive a seven-mile road to a parking lot. From there you can walk the fully paved, one-mile round trip up and down to the observation tower.

Second, timing. Clingmans Dome is open year-round, but the Dome Road is only open April 1–November 30.

Next, conditions. Because of its steep 13% incline, Clingmans Dome can be considered moderately difficult for some. It might be a more strenuous hike for the elderly or those not as physically fit, but there are benches along the half-mile trail to take a breather. Also, you may need to bring a jacket because the air is about 20 degrees cooler at the top than at the bottom.

Last, resources. Entrance to Great Smoky Mountains National Park is free. Your only cost is your time, gas money, and maybe a stay at a cabin or a camping site.[18]

Have you gotten the analogy yet? Everest = billionaire. Clingmans Dome = millionaire. Couch = neither. So, to say this another way . . . doing nothing—sitting on your couch—is mathematically closer to millionaire than millionaire is to billionaire. But for those of us who didn't grow up wealthy, we tend to emotionally put billionaire and millionaire close together on the spectrum, which makes wealth *feel* unattainable.

The reason I'm beating this drum so hard and loud is that it's critical for you to understand how possible it is to become a millionaire! There are only about 614 billionaires in the U.S.,[19] but there are approximately twelve million millionaires.[20] Becoming a millionaire isn't a treacherous, death-defying hike. It's a planned walk up an incline that might require a jacket and maybe a breather on a bench. And you can do it!

A Baby Steps Millionaire Looks a Lot Like You

When we set out to do Ramsey's *National Study of Millionaires,* we wanted to do three things:

1. Make it clear to people that the Baby Steps are a wealth-building plan, not just a get-out-of-debt plan like some had narrowly defined it in the marketplace.
2. Identify just who the typical millionaire is, their lifestyle and habits, so that people could see themselves in the characteristics and see how attainable the millionaire milestone is.
3. Prove that **anyone** can be a millionaire and inspire **anyone** to be a millionaire.

Plus, it had been more than twenty years since Thomas Stanley and William Danko had shaken up the neighborhood and destroyed people's misconceptions about wealth and the wealthy with their landmark study and book, *The Millionaire Next Door*. At that time, I'd been teaching the Baby Steps long enough to start seeing the wealth-building results in people's lives. These were normal, everyday folks who had worked the Baby Steps, gotten out of debt, started investing, and had become millionaires. They kept showing up—emailing us, coming to live events, calling in to the radio show, telling us their incredible stories of how "this stuff really works!" In fact, that's what prompted our Everyday Millionaire Theme Hour segment on the show.

So, we dug in with more than ten thousand millionaires from all across the country. And we found out they have a lot of the same tendencies and characteristics. You can read the complete study in the Appendix, but I want to highlight a few here to show you just how much they look like YOU . . .

- 88% have a four-year degree.
- 62% graduated from public state schools.
- 8% attended community college.
- 9% never graduated college at all.
- Almost half of the millionaires had a B average or lower in school.
- 40% were involved in sports/cheerleading (the most common extracurricular activity).
- Only 31% averaged $100K household income a year.
- Only 7% averaged over $200K over the course of their career.
- 96% enjoy what they do for a career.
- 64% say they "loved" their jobs.
- 94% of millionaires live on less than they make, compared to 55% of the general population.

It's like looking in a mirror, right? See, I told you that *YOU CAN DO IT TOO!* We're not talking Bezos Billionaire Steps. Those aren't for everybody. We're talking Baby Steps, and they *are* for everybody. They're for YOU and the life and legacy YOU want to create. You can do this! You can be a millionaire. The Baby Steps will get you there.

CHAPTER 5

Belief versus Barriers

She couldn't believe she'd done it. Jackie was a finalist in the Lieutenant Governor's writing contest! As a middle schooler, it was the most exciting thing that had happened in Jackie's life. Her dad was always too busy working to be involved in her schoolwork, so she often had to figure things out herself. That's why Jackie was even more proud to be among the contest finalists—and a little scared. She worried that her dad would have to work one of his two jobs and wouldn't be able to take her to the event where they would announce the winner. She also worried that she'd have nothing to wear to a fancy event with the Lieutenant Governor.

She begged her dad to go. She even enlisted her older sister to beg on her behalf. Finally, he gave in. And he somehow scraped together enough money for a nice new dress for her to wear. This was a big deal because she and her siblings only got new clothes at the start of a school year—and even then, it was only one new top and one new pair of pants. The rest of their clothes were dreaded hand-me-downs passed between many siblings. But this dress was *brand-new*—a turquoise dream with a skirt of four layers—and it made Jackie feel fancy (even if it was purchased from a discount store).

Although she didn't win the top writer award, Jackie felt proud during the special event. Because, for a moment, she was just like all the other kids . . . she was at a school event with her parent. She felt like she'd won just by having her dad there with her.

By the world's standards, Jackie wasn't "just like all the other kids." Jackie is an African American woman who grew up in poverty and was the fifth of six kids in her family. Her dad was a single parent who had custody of all six kids after a divorce from Jackie's mom. At the time of the divorce, Jackie was in elementary school, so it wasn't until much later in life that she realized how unusual this arrangement was.

Jackie's dad only had a sixth-grade education and worked at a textile mill where they made jeans. He also worked a second side job with a construction company to help make ends meet. Even though her dad didn't talk about money much with the family, there was an unspoken understanding of how tough it was to feed, clothe, and house six kids on a factory worker's salary.

Jackie and her siblings grew up in a two-bedroom ranch home located along a dirt road in a small rural town. She and her three sisters slept in one room with two twin beds—two girls to each twin. Her dad slept in the other bedroom. Both of her brothers slept on a bed that took up half of the family room. Even though they were poor and could barely make ends meet, Jackie's dad was a proud man and didn't receive food stamps, welfare, or any other form of public assistance for his family except for having his kids take part in the school's free lunch program.

Unfortunately, Jackie's dad didn't make it to her last school event. He never got to see her or her younger sister graduate from high school. A few months before Jackie walked across the stage to receive her diploma, he passed away from cancer. He was just forty-nine years old. From then on, Jackie was on her own—but not without a foundation of life lessons he had taught her. She credits him for her early understanding of money and for teaching her how to work hard, stay away from debt, and treat people right.

Even though she felt like the deck was stacked against her, Jackie didn't just stand still and let being parentless or poverty-stricken paralyze her. She went on from high school and got her bachelor's degree in communications. Though she did take out about $8,000 in student loans, she worked forty-plus hours per week at a large department store so she wouldn't go further in debt. Her grades weren't exactly what she wanted them to be, but she was committed to working full-time to avoid taking out any more loans.

After Jackie graduated from college, she remained with the same department store, working in communications at the regional headquarters for a starting salary of $15,000. She got married, and shortly after, she and her husband moved to another state for his job. She was able to stay with the same store chain as an assistant manager in their new city. She and her husband had a daughter about a year later. Jackie eventually left retail and started working in sales for a data analytics company in the area. Everything was going well—two working parents, two incomes, one wonderful daughter. And then it all took a turn.

In 2004, Jackie and her husband divorced after ten years of marriage. Like many divorce situations, it was an extremely tough time and a huge financial wake-up call. Jackie's biggest fear was that she would find herself in the pit of poverty again—and drag her young daughter down right along with her. She remembered how hard her childhood was having no money and how devastating it was always having to go without—no phone, no new clothes, and every Thursday before payday, no food in the refrigerator.

She thought a lot about how to make sure she and her daughter would not be a statistic. She had read a study once that said a Black, single mom is one of the most likely demographics to be in poverty. Jackie was determined to make sure she and her daughter didn't become that statistic. As she settled her divorce, she wanted a clean slate. She took around $7,000 from her savings and knocked out her car loan, student loan, and credit card quickly. She was focused and motivated to keep poverty in her rearview mirror and give her daughter a better life than she had growing up.

Shortly after the divorce, Jackie discovered *The Ramsey Show* podcast and the Baby Steps. It confirmed for her that she was indeed on the right track by getting out of debt, and it gave her confidence to tackle her finances in a simple, organized way moving forward. She remembers listening to a call I took on the radio show from a widow who was trying to get her life together after the passing of her husband. Even though Jackie's spouse hadn't died, she was dealing with the death of her marriage. She was encouraged by what I told the widow: *Take some time to just breathe before you make any major decisions.*

Jackie followed that advice and took time to get her feet under her and heal emotionally. Thankfully, she had a stable job with benefits making about $50,000 a year and was receiving about $800 per month in court-ordered child support. She was also diligent to not accumulate more debt.

A couple of years later, Jackie started working the Baby Steps. It took her about two years to build her fully funded emergency fund to $20,000, which covered about five months of expenses. That was really important to her because it meant security for her and her daughter. Once she reached this point, she went all in on Baby Step 4. She kept a rein on her budget but began to build a comfortable middle-class lifestyle—something she had only dreamed of when she was growing up. She could afford for her daughter to participate in sports, and she was able to increase her 401(k) contributions to 10% instead of just doing the company match of 6%. She also started maxing out her Roth IRA, which put her at our recommended 15%.

By 2008, she was able to max out all of her tax-advantaged accounts: 401(k), Roth IRA, and HSA. Turns out, this was jet fuel for the growth of her net worth. In 2013, just five years later, her salary in sales hit $78,000, and she realized she was halfway to becoming a millionaire!

She discovered this by creating what she calls her "net worth statement." Basically, she plugged all her numbers into a spreadsheet to keep track of what she owned minus what she owed. She listed categories in different columns: type of savings or investment account, provider, date started, starting amount, current amount, mortgage debt amount. It was motivating for her to update it every month and see how her net worth was growing as she was paying down her mortgage and maxing out her savings and investing accounts. She started making projections of how much her net worth would grow based on what she was contributing to her accounts, the estimated growth of the accounts, and how quickly she was paying down her mortgage. In fact, she said creating a net worth statement was one of the most powerful exercises she had ever done with her finances.

She wasn't kidding! By 2018—just another five years later—her sales income was $89,000 and she hit the $1.2 million mark with no debt except her mortgage. Did you catch that? As a Black, single mom who grew up in poverty, Jackie put herself through college, got rid of debt, and grew her income from $15,000 to about $81,000 (her ten-year average income in sales). She saved and maxed her investments to reach a $1.2 million net worth in just ten years! This is how it shaped up:

- $600,000 in a 401(k) invested in mutual funds
- $400,000 in an IRA with a mix of mutual funds and stock
- $100,000 in an HSA (Health Savings Account)
- $100,000 in her home's equity.

Despite all the systemic barriers that were seemingly in her way and despite receiving zero inheritance, Jackie found a way to reach $1.2 million by age forty-nine! Not only that, but she retired at age forty-nine too! It's stunning—maybe even redemptive—to think that was the same age her dad was when he died. Jackie calls herself an "unlikely millionaire." But in my estimation, she's every bit a "likely millionaire" because of two very important factors: the Baby Steps and her belief.

I asked Jackie what advice she would give to the twenty-three-year-old version of herself. She said, "You really have to have the right mindset. Once you decide becoming a millionaire is possible, the steps are pretty simple. Get your income up, get your debt down, increase your savings rate, and invest on a regular basis." In other words, she started believing she could do it, and then took the steps to make it happen. She opened her mind to the possibilities beyond the poverty of her childhood, beyond the fear she experienced with her divorce, and beyond the systemic barriers the world said were in her way.

Jackie's now in her fifties and has grown her net worth to $1.5 million, including an extra $50,000 in her home's equity. She's working toward a master's degree to fulfill a dream she's had since she made her so-called "pitiful grades" during her undergrad years. Even though she was proud of being a first-generation college grad, she had always known she was capable of doing much better academically and wanted to reclaim that experience. Not only did she hit the mark with a 4.0 GPA, Jackie was also able to fund her master's program using leftover money from her daughter's 529 College Savings Plan.

The graphic design program her daughter was enrolled in at a local community college ended up costing much less than Jackie anticipated, so both mom and daughter were able to go to college debt-free. Talk about believing you can change your family tree! Jackie got it done with highest honors! I'm proud of her, and I know her dad would be proud of the intelligent, financially independent woman she's become too.

Don't Quit Before You Start

Jackie is a hero! Her story is awesome and inspiring for all of us. But imagine what it would have been like if she hadn't believed it was possible. Unbelief sounds a lot like:

I can't do this.

The deck is stacked against me.

I have nothing, not even my parents.

I can't afford rent, let alone college.

It's too much. There's no reason to even try.

What would Jackie's life have looked like if she didn't think she stood a chance? What choices would she have made? Is it likely she would be a millionaire today? Sadly, no.

Belief matters.

Hope matters.

A lot.

To be without belief or hope is a really sad place. It can blind us and keep us trapped in the fear and lies of a victim mentality. But belief gives us courage and confidence and causes us to act. You can do *most* things if you simply believe and don't quit before you start. Believing you can is more than half the battle when you set out to begin anything new. This isn't the same as believing you can do *anything*—because that isn't true either. Belief or positive thinking is powerful, but it's not necessarily a cure-all. It doesn't always change the circumstance you're in. And it won't cause you to suddenly possess skills or attributes that you simply do not have.

I know a woman whose son has been a goal-setter basically since he could pronounce the word *goal*. In his middle school years, he wrote lists of the goals he wanted to reach in sports, like shooting and making ten thousand basketball shots on his driveway hoop by the end of summer. Most of the time he kept a notebook tracking his goals and progress. But sometimes he'd hang Post-it notes on his bulletin board, bathroom mirror, or other parts of the house as reminders. One day when his mom was walking through the kitchen, she saw a bright yellow Post-it note hanging on the family chalkboard. In her son's handwriting it read: *5 ft. by June 1.* He had set a goal to grow taller so he could better compete on the basketball court with boys in his class who had hit their growth spurts sooner than he had. Of course, he knew it wasn't possible to wish himself tall. But it didn't stop him from measuring himself every week until he reached five feet tall.

I'm definitely over five feet tall, but I'm not over six feet tall. I am over sixty years old, so my growth spurt ended a long, long time ago. And I realize no amount of positive thinking is going to make me tall. I also have a reasonable level of intelligence, but there is no evidence that I am intellectually gifted, and that is not something that I can grow. I am simply not a genius, so if that's what would have been required for me to build wealth, I wouldn't have made it.

Lots of people seem to have an unfair head start on their wealth-building journey. That's because everyone has a different starting line. There are a lot of broken things in our culture and our systems—A LOT of systemic problems. Sexism is real. Racism is real. Education access is unequal. Broken, dysfunctional families are the norm. But the starting line is not the question. The only question is: Are the problems big enough to hold you back? Are they big enough to keep you from winning? If you believe The System or The Man is holding all the cards and there's no possible way you can win, then you won't engage in the sacrificial behaviors required to win. You won't even think about starting down the Baby Steps path. The only important discussion, then, is The Finish Line and whether or not you believe you can and will do what it takes to reach it.

If someone believes that the game is rigged, that the systems of our culture will simply not allow them to build wealth and become a Baby Steps Millionaire, then they would be insane to sacrifice to win. A sane person will never sacrifice to win at a goal they truly believe they cannot achieve. To save, invest, budget, or pay off debt would be silly if you think it's not going to work.

Belief matters . . . A LOT. Henry Ford said, "Whether you think you can or you think you can't, you're right." Jackie saw her dad work two jobs and avoid debt. She listened to people do their Debt-Free Screams on *The Ramsey Show* and knew it could be done. These examples grew her belief that she could take control of her personal finances. And when it came time to act on her belief, she was able to do the hard things, make the hard decisions to climb out of poverty and never slip back, even when divorce threatened her financial situation.

"When I was younger, I didn't even think this was possible. I thought there was no way I could do it," Jackie told me during our Everyday Millionaires Theme Hour. "But once I got my head around it, I told myself, *I can do this. It doesn't matter where I came from, and it doesn't matter how I was brought up.* I realized if I follow these steps and do these things, I can get there just like anybody else."

Outside forces are all around us trying to take us down left and right, but they don't stand a chance against someone who is filled with belief, desire, and hope. I don't care where your starting line is, you can do this wealth-building thing! I know you can because I have met you thousands of times in the last thirty years. I know you can because Ramsey's *National Study of Millionaires* revealed that the typical Everyday Millionaire comes from every possible background, race, creed, color, and national origin. They are not all middle-aged white guys coming from privileged homes. That premise is a lie, and because it steals hope and spreads hopelessness, it is evil.

The study actually refutes a lot of the common lies people believe and stereotypes people have about millionaires. Contrary to what most people think, Baby Steps Millionaires don't only come from bigwig, high-paying jobs or career fields. In small-town America seventy-five years ago, the starting line to be "well to do" was to have a job as a banker, lawyer, or doctor. This was true so often that the stereotype was embedded into our cultural psyche: to be wealthy you must be in one of those types of fields. But our study showed a surprising shift in this thinking from then to now. Instead, the top five jobs of Everyday Millionaires came out like this:

1. Engineer
2. Accountant
3. Teacher

4. Management
5. Attorney

It's interesting to note that medical doctor did not make the top five and neither did banker. And attorney only made the bottom of the top-five list. Possibly the most inspiring is that teacher made the list at number three. Teacher! You might be shocked, but I've seen this over and over again. I've gotten to meet a large number of Baby Steps Millionaires over the years and many of them are teachers and police officers. Kind of messes with the stereotypes, doesn't it?

It's also interesting to note that among the millionaires in management that landed in the number four spot, only 15% were in senior management and only 7% were C-suite executives. What this shows is that titles and career paths don't mean squat as to whether or not someone will become a millionaire. In fact, 18% of all Everyday Millionaires are self-employed and make up their own titles and career paths. Nope, it's not about titles or career paths at all. It's not even about how much money you make! Yes, you read that right. One of our most surprising findings in the study was that 33% of millionaires NEVER had a six-figure household income. But is it really *that* surprising since teachers are number three on the list? I mean, how many teachers do you know who make over six figures?

So, if specific titles, career paths, and salaries don't make you a millionaire, what does? Think back to what we learned in Jackie's story. The two most important factors in becoming a millionaire are: belief and the Baby Steps.

So, let's talk some more about the power of belief. Of the over ten thousand million-aires who participated in the study, 97% said they believe they ultimately control their own destiny. In the same survey, only 69% of the general public said they believe they ultimately control their own destiny. That's a big distinction! It shows that belief really matters to the process of becoming a millionaire.

Another big distinction is the undeniable financial success legal immigrants have as compared to native-born Americans. For instance, 40% of Fortune 500 companies were founded by immigrants or the children of immigrants.[21] And even beyond household name companies, immigrant entrepreneurs have made a huge impact on the American economy, according to research done by The Kauffman Foundation:

- Immigrants started 28.5% of all new U.S. businesses in 2014.

- Between 2006 and 2012, immigrants founded one quarter of the engineering and technology companies in the U.S.

- In 2012, immigrant-founded engineering and technology firms employed approximately 560,000 workers and generated $63 billion in sales.

- Immigrants have seen their rate of business generation rise by more than 50% since the start of the new millennium, while native-born citizens have seen their rate of new-business generation decline by 10%.

- Immigrants are now more than twice as likely to start a business than native-born citizens.[22]

It seems obvious that immigrants have more to overcome in order to be successful, not less—more racism, more language barriers, and more cultural misunderstandings. But in spite of starting further back in the race, they successfully cross the finish line more often. Why is that? Because belief matters.

I can't help but think that as these immigrants dreamed about America before they left their home country, all they wanted and believed for was a chance. All they wanted was freedom. All they wanted was to be greeted by the famous Statue of Liberty and all the opportunity she stands for. I can imagine them contemplating what they would do with their newfound opportunity, thinking some version of: *Just put me in the game, Coach, and I'll leave it all on the field.* Every night as their head hit the pillow, they must have hoped: *America might not give me a guarantee, but it will give me a chance—the best chance I can have.* Then when they got to America, the statistics say they took that chance, believed, worked, sacrificed, and succeeded. They found that the belief they carried across oceans and borders played a huge part in their millionaire-making success—that believing you can win is actually essential to winning. Belief matters.

It's Not Where You Come From, It's Where You're Going

All the Jackies who've become millionaires out from the depths of poverty, all the immigrants who've become millionaires out from the snares of opportunity-deficient countries—they've discovered the most important thing: It's not about where you come from. It's about where you're going. It's not your situation—it's your response to your situation.

Former Secretary of State Condoleezza Rice knows this truth all too well. She grew up in segregated Alabama at a time during the Civil Rights Movement when racial tensions were high all across the city of Birmingham, including her middle-class neighborhood. In fact, the violence was so rampant during this time, Birmingham was given the nickname "Bombingham." Condoleezza was just nine years old when one of her schoolmates was among the four Black girls killed in the infamous 1963 bombing of Sixteenth Street Baptist Church.[23] She remembers it being a scary time in her childhood.[24]

However, Condoleezza's parents did not allow her to focus on the violence and the barriers of race, gender, economics, or education. They taught her that there are no victims—even in an unfair climate. They instilled in her this mantra: "The minute you think of yourself as a victim, you've given control of your life to somebody else. And you might not be able to control your circumstances, but you can control your response to your circumstances, so don't you ever think of yourself as a victim."[25]

This belief shaped Condoleezza's life in profound ways. Neither her race, gender, economic background, nor her segregated education stopped her from becoming the first Black woman to serve as the National Security Adviser, the first Black woman to serve as Secretary of State, and the first Black woman to serve as Provost of Stanford University.[26] Her accomplishments are extraordinary and her mindset even more so. She truly lives what she believes: "It doesn't matter where you came from; it matters where you're going."[27]

Bust through the Barriers

If you've made it to this halfway point in the book and you're still reading, we both know where you're going—or at least where you want to go. You want to be a millionaire. To that I would say, right now, today, your life is a reflection of what you wanted yesterday. That's right. **You have what you want**.

Now, it might feel like I just turned the dial up a notch. Those five words can feel like a smack right between the eyes. They did for me too, decades ago when I came to the same realization. It's a hard pill to swallow, but it's true. **You have what you want**. Just let that sink in.

Right now, your situation reflects your desires and your choices. If you're stuck, **you have what you want**. If all you see right now are ignorant and unforgiving obstacles in front, behind, or all around you, then you're seeing what you want to see and **you have what you want** amidst those obstacles. If you're sprinting forward despite those obstacles, **you have what you want**. If you wanted something bad enough, you'd have it. I'll say it again, **you have what you want.** So, what do you want? What do you believe is possible?

I had ignorant and unforgiving obstacles in my path too. I've experienced my own set of stereotypes. I am a hillbilly and proud of it. But I've been judged as stupid because I'm from the South and have a Southern drawl. For years, executives in the radio business thought I broadcast my show from a double-wide trailer in overalls and no shoes because we're located in Tennessee, not the East Coast.

Everyone has an -ism or a stereotype they have to bust through. Everyone has some unfair advantage standing in their way. Bill Gates is smarter than me. Steve Jobs knows more about computers than me. George Clooney is prettier than me. So what? This is the hand I've been dealt, so I'm playing my hand. I don't fixate on the obstacles. And I certainly don't let them dictate what I believe is possible for me and my situation.

I'm generally optimistic about our world. Eeyore has never been my spirit animal. I don't think the biggest problem we have today is structural or systemic. The biggest problem we have today is a breakdown in belief. People are believing the wrong things. And when you believe the wrong things, you make bad decisions because your worldview is screwed up. When someone with a big heart decries the injustices of our culture in an effort to change the culture, I applaud them. However, some people spend so much time focusing on the big barriers and problems of our culture that they become convinced "regular folks" cannot overcome their barriers, so they peddle hopelessness. Selling hopelessness to move a social agenda forward is evil because it robs "regular folks" of their belief that they can win. But if you can believe that what happens in your house is more important for your quality of life over the next several decades than what happens in the White House—or your neighbor's house, or your enemy's house for that matter—then you *can* bust through the hopelessness and the barriers and embrace belief once and for all!

Be a Victor Not a Victim

Remember what Condoleezza said: You're not a victim of your circumstance. It doesn't matter where you came from or what your situation is. You can control your response.

The worst year of my life, I made $6,000. Boy, that sucked. I was a victim of the tax law change under the Reagan administration. So, did Ronald Reagan ruin my life? Nope. Did Congress ruin my life? Did the IRS ruin my life? Did the banks ruin my life? I went bankrupt because of all of them and the moves they made. And I also went bankrupt because of the moves I made that put me in the firing lines. That meant when all those idiots pulled the trigger, I got shot. But I was the one who stepped in front of those bullets, so I was asking for it. Sure, I was ignorant and didn't know any better. That was thirty years ago. So, am I a victim or not?

It's worth repeating: Ninety-seven percent of the over ten thousand millionaires we surveyed said they believe they ultimately control their own destiny. In math class, we call that statistically significant. Believing that there's still a chance, still an opportunity, still abundance available for you will keep you from a victim mentality, from paralysis and resignation, from envy and jealousy, from greed and entitlement. Belief will cause you to have what you want!

C. S. Lewis said, "You can't go back and change the beginning, but you can start where you are and change the ending." You get to decide the finish line. You are not a victim. You can control the controllables. A victim of circumstances is someone who decides to sit down and stay in the circumstances. All of us have had bad things done to us, said about us, happen to us. And at that moment, we were a victim. But if you remain in that victim state, you will not progress and become successful in any area of your life—your parenting, your marriage, your career, your spiritual walk, your physical condition, or your wealth building. In anything you do, you have to decide: *I am not a victim. I control my destiny.*

And here's a special word of warning about choosing not to be a victim: Be careful who you hang out with. The Bible says in 1 Corinthians 15:33, "Do not be deceived. Bad company ruins good morals" (ESV). You become who you hang around with. If you hang out with people who are stuck, unmotivated, and negative, guess what you'll be? You need to hang out with people who believe that it's possible to build wealth. You need to spend time with people who are wise with their money, people who are goal-oriented, people who have a purpose and know where they're going in life. This should be part of your financial plan, whether you're on Baby Step 1 or Baby Step 7.

There's even science that suggests it's likely your income will be influenced by the incomes represented in your social network. Dr. Nicholas Christakis and Dr. James Fowler conducted the first major study done on the scope of social influence by using the data set from the Framingham Heart Study, one of the largest and longest running health studies ever. They analyzed the nature and extent of person-to-person spread of obesity. Say what? Yes, the evidence proved that you can in effect "spread" obesity.[28]

According to their findings, you are 45% more likely than random chance to gain weight over the next two to four years if a friend of yours becomes obese. But even more shocking, your likelihood to gain weight increases by 20% if a friend of your friend becomes obese—even if you don't know that friend of a friend! And believe it or not, the weight gain extends by one more person. The study showed that you're 10% more likely than random chance to gain weight if a friend of the friend of your friend is obese. Christakis and Fowler found that a strong explanation for this is normalizing. Your perception of acceptable body size and behavior will adjust accordingly if the circles of friends around you are obese.

With the same data, Christakis and Fowler found similar results with friends who smoke. You are 61% more likely to be a smoker if your friend smokes. One more friend extended makes you 29% more likely to smoke. And one more friend from there makes you 11% more likely.

Just like the spread of obesity and smoking behaviors, Christakis and Fowler also found that the spread of happiness reaches up to three degrees of separation as well.[29] You're 15% more likely to be happy if your friend is happy, 10% if your friend's friend is happy, and 6% if a friend of a friend of your friend is happy.

Understanding how powerful and extensive your social influence can be, it only makes sense that who you hang out with will have an effect on your financial journey. It should make you take an accounting and ask yourself: *Are my closest friends (and their friends) successfully building wealth? Do they believe it's possible or are they playing the victim of their circumstances?* Part of growing your belief that you can build wealth is hanging out with people who believe it and are doing it.

Mike Todd, an American film producer, said, "I've never been poor, only broke. Being poor is a frame of mind. Being broke is a temporary situation." Sometimes the biggest obstacle we can face is between our own two ears—our state of mind. Poor is a state of mind. Belief is also a state of mind. Either one can shape how all of your brain power, knowledge, passion, and energy converge and cause you to act. A victim state of mind will cause you to have an excuse not to win. A belief state of mind will cause you to do everything it takes to win. Belief will cause you to overcome. Belief will cause you to be the hero of your own story.

I want my brothers and sisters from every race, gender, economic, and educational background to hear me loud and clear: Being successful requires perseverance and an unwavering belief that transcends any barriers and stupid people in your way, but success is truly possible for everyone. You *can* become a Baby Steps Millionaire. Choose to believe.

CHAPTER 6

The Quickest Right Way to a Million

T he second-rate hotel ballroom was poorly lit. The chairs were too close together. The place was jam-packed with every type of human you can imagine. Poorly dressed and dressed-for-success people in every shape, size, and color. I mean, this place was wild! There was an excitement in the air, an urgency, even a palpable expectation that you could almost taste and smell.

Of course, for dramatic effect, the pre-show music blared loudly over the chintzy hotel sound system in an effort to amp the audience with songs like the *Rocky* theme song, *Gonna Fly Now,* and Queen's *We Are the Champions*. The keynote speaker was intentionally delayed, making his stage entrance late to build the tension.

For the next hour, he told a room packed full of mainly broke people how we could all get rich buying real estate with "nothing down." It was good that we could do it with "nothing down" because that was precisely what I had for a down payment—NOTHING! He gave us example after example and four different financing techniques to get a loan for even more than we would pay for the house. I found out later that two of those four techniques were criminal fraud and never used them. (In case you're wondering: Having one contract with the seller and a different contract that you show the bank is called *dual contracts* and is criminal fraud.) But that didn't stop this room full of wild characters from getting jacked up to believe it was going to be easy to get rich in real estate with "nothing down." And then, right on cue and in the most annoying tell-them-what-they've-won game show host voice, the evening ended with: *Aaaannnd ... if you're really serious about real estate investing, you can sign up for a weekend-long course where you'll learn not just four techniques, but over fifty proven methods of getting rich in real estate that will virtually guarantee your future success! Aaaannnd ... for tonight only, it could all be yours—for the low, low price of $3,500!*

Yep, that wacky night back in 1983 I endured my first infomercial, long before infomercials were even a thing. I was twenty-three years old, and as much as it still makes me wince to think about, I got enticed by the nothing-down concept. I did not sign up for the weekend class, but I left that room and within a few weeks, I bought my first house with, you guessed it, nothing down. As I mentioned before, over the next several years, I bought millions in real estate. I flipped a lot of it for profit and held $4 million worth of property with $3 million worth of debt, making my net worth $1 million—my first million. At twenty-six years old, I was a millionaire. I had done it! I had gotten rich quick! I made $250,000 that year. That was a lot of money then—even a lot of money now. But ... it was all a house of cards.

At the time, I didn't really know I was building a house of cards. Like so many in the early '80s, I was just caught up in the nothing-down real estate investing craze that swept across the nation. I was engrossed in the frenzied pace that comes with getting rich quick. I wasn't behind with anyone or late on any payments. But I had so much debt. I kept almost no cash, and the bank ruled my life. Then the bank got sold to another bank. I had a lot of short-term notes, and the bank called them all because I was an idiot who signed up and gave them the right to! And just as fast as it had been built, my house of cards fell. I lost everything. I was appalled and shocked, but I shouldn't have been because guess what a house of cards does? It falls! Every time. There's no such thing as a well-constructed house of cards. It's fragile. It's volatile. It falls flat. Every. Single. Time.

And yet, as perilous as it is, the pull of getting rich quick is powerful. At the time, I belonged to a real estate investors club where over one hundred others had followed the exact same model for buying property pitched in that ballroom and other ballrooms all over America. What's interesting to note is that, of everyone who persisted in using these high-leverage techniques, I don't know a single soul today who didn't go broke. Even the guy who wrote the book *Nothing Down* filed Chapter 11 bankruptcy!

What is it about us humans that makes us want something for nothing? There must be something spiritually broken in us that makes us lose our minds at the thought of easy money. Me too. I started this chapter with my personal story about falling into a stupid, easy-money hole of my own! Like I said in Chapter 1, when building wealth, everyone wants the highest probability of success and the fastest turnaround time. The hard pill to swallow is that there's one right way and all kinds of wrong ways to go about it.

The Quickest Wrong Ways to a Million

We yearn for a shortcut, a quick and easy answer. We want Instant Pots, not Crockpots. We go crazy for the lottery. All across the country, we spend billions every year on lottery tickets, looking to get instantly rich. We want an effortless, lucrative stock trade from an easy internet tip. We want to buy the Iraqi dinar because it's poised to go exponential. Bitcoin, short selling stock, margin plays, commodities, gold, silver, mercury, an oil well, baseball cards, coins, purchasing a Picasso at a garage sale for $10, and of course, my all-time favorite . . . Beanie Babies. Yep, Beanie Babies! You may not be old enough to remember in the early '90s when the Ty company changed the investing world with stuffed animals, but some otherwise sane people actually began collecting Beanie Babies as an investment. Back then I took way too many calls on my radio show from people who were very angry with me for suggesting that Beanie Babies as an investment for their kid's college fund was *Stupid* with a capital "S."

We want to be an overnight success. Things like reality TV and Instagram make us believe we can. I can't help but laugh a bit endearingly at this, because since my bankruptcy, I've wised up and worked my butt off for thirty years to be "an overnight success." Yet how many times have we seen a young athlete, singer, or actor hit their rise to stardom, get a bunch of money, and then a few short months or years later their lives are completely destroyed? Sadly, there are too many to count! Take pro football players for instance.

The odds of a high school player making it to the NFL is a 0.2% chance.[30] But still young players dream of making salaries like Patrick Mahomes, quarterback for the Kansas City Chiefs. In 2021, he earned a salary of $24.81 million dollars.[31] But for all the highly paid players, there are also a bunch of rookies who earned the league minimum of $660,000. So, if you were to average out all the salaries across the NFL, it would work out to about $1 to $1.5 million dollars per player.[32] (If you think that's high, NBA players make an average salary of $9.5 million dollars a year!)[33] But a million is only a million if you can make it and keep it. Many pro athletes have learned the "keeping it" part is harder than they ever thought.

In 2009, the sports world was alarmed to read Pablo Torre's article in *Sports Illustrated* stating that:

- By the time they have been retired for two years, 78% of former NFL players have gone bankrupt or are under financial stress because of joblessness or divorce.
- Within five years of retirement, an estimated 60% of former NBA players are broke.[34]

Six years later, in 2015, the National Bureau of Economic Research reported that almost 16% of NFL players filed bankruptcy within twelve years of retiring.[35]

In their *30 for 30* documentary "Broke," ESPN told the stories of NFL players who had made millions in their careers but found themselves with nothing left after they retired. The film included story after story of players' bad investments, greedy family members, medical issues, and extravagant lifestyles. One of the athletes featured in the documentary was Andre Rison.

Andre was twenty-two years old when he was drafted by the Indianapolis Colts in 1989. He only played with the Colts for one season before being traded to the Atlanta Falcons where, in just five years, he became a huge star as a dominant receiver. He went on to play for the Cleveland Browns, Green Bay Packers, Jacksonville Jaguars, Kansas City Chiefs, Oakland Raiders, and the CFL's Toronto Argonauts. Over the course of his twelve-year career, he earned a Super Bowl ring with the Packers and racked up almost seven hundred fifty catches, eighty-four touchdowns, and over 10,200 yards. He also earned over $20 million in salary and endorsements over his career.

But Andre loved to spend money. In the documentary, he said, "I guarantee I spent a million dollars on jewelry." In addition to jewelry, Andre was known to go clubbing with an entourage of forty to forty-five people. He said, "We were going to new levels. . . . I'd be lying on the bed knocked out (after getting back from the club) with $10,000 lying on the floor. I've got another $5,000 in my pocket. You might find another $7,500 in the pocket in my coat."[36]

Andre's terrible financial decisions finally caught up with him. With a huge pile of unpaid child support bills, he declared bankruptcy in 2007. He has managed to turn his life around and get going in the right direction. In 2020, his net worth was back to $250,000[37]—but it's still a far cry from the $20 million dollars he made during his career.

Whether you're a sports fan or not, you can clearly see the power and peril of getting rich quick in Andre's story. And it doesn't just happen to young, ill-equipped jocks. How many times have you heard of someone who's never had money in their whole life get lucky and win the lottery? All that easy money usually destroys them.

It breaks my heart to see news stories come across my desk about lottery winners who won millions and then were ruthlessly scammed by relatives, those who used their winnings for drugs and ended up in jail, those who bought houses and cars they could not afford, those who ended up bankrupt and living out their retirement in trailer parks, those with tragic stories like Billie Bob Harrell, Jr.

Billie Bob was a forty-seven-year-old man from Texas who quit his job at Home Depot after winning $31 million in the Texas Lotto jackpot. He bought a ranch and was generous with his winnings, giving big donations to his church and buying homes for family members. But just twenty months after he claimed the winning ticket, he was broke and broken by the weight of the wealth he'd come by so quickly. He ended up putting a shotgun to his chest and pulling the trigger. The *Houston Press* reported that shortly before his death, Harrell told a financial adviser: "Winning the lottery is the worst thing that ever happened to me."[38]

Getting rich quick can be more of a curse than a blessing. I'm not saying you're bad or evil to get money quickly. But the Bible warns us, and there's obviously a ton of social proof all around us, that there are all kinds of problems that can happen when lots of money comes into our lives too quickly. Why is that? Well, as most of us are growing our wealth, we're also emotionally and spiritually maturing. We are growing as individuals as our money grows. In a way, this simultaneous growth protects us. As we gradually build both our wealth and our character at the same time, our wealth never gets so big that it crushes us because our character is strong enough to carry it.

Time and Diligence

I learned this the hard way. My first million crushed me because I hadn't yet developed the character and faith strong enough to carry it. When I share my story, I often say that I met God on the way up, but I got to know Him on the way down. This is not just some quippy line I say for fun. It's the excruciatingly hard truth of that very vulnerable time in my life. From my knees, I dug into scripture to understand how to do this money thing better—to find out what *God* says about it, not how *Dave* thinks it should go. Turns out, He's got a lot to say about money and about the time and diligence it takes to build it. There are several scriptures in the book of Proverbs alone that give us the truth about getting rich quick. Let's take a look at two of my favorites.

Proverbs 28:20 says, "A faithful man will abound with blessings, but he who hastens to be rich will not go unpunished" (NKJV). This scripture is dead-on, straight-up truth. A person with a slow and steady, predictable approach over time will overflow with abundance. But a person with a get-rich-quick method will get smashed, just like I did. You can get wealth in a lot of ways. You can get sudden fame. You can hit the lottery. One in a bazillion people do. But the rest of us who are trying to get wealth quickly will get punished. And the punishment is losing your money—or worse, your soul. In other words, the quickest way to get rich quick is . . . don't.

Proverbs 13:11 tells us, "Wealth gained hastily will dwindle, but whoever gathers little by little will increase it" (ESV). We don't use the words "hastens" or "hastily" too much in our language anymore, but what do they mean? You're in too big of a freaking hurry to get rich quick—that's what they mean! This verse is saying wealth gained quickly will fade away; it won't last. But people who gather wealth little by little will multiply it. I personally like the way The Message version hits the nail on the head: "Easy come, easy go, but steady diligence pays off." Diligently investing your money, little by little over time is where real, lasting wealth comes from. Simply put, the best way to get rich quick is to get rich slow.

The Quickest Right Way to a Million

Beverly Sills, a famous opera singer, reminds us, "There is no shortcut to any place worth going." Our data from *The National Study of Millionaires* indicates that almost no millionaires get there quick or easy with one big hit. Only 3% received an inheritance of $1 million or more. And only 2% of millionaires surveyed said they came from an upper-income family. Not only that, but three out of four millionaires (75%) said that regular, consistent investing over a long period of time is the reason for their success. In other words, they became wealthy slow and steady, not quick and flashy.

And still, most Baby Steps Millionaires who work the 7-step plan, reach the millionaire mark in twenty years or less from the very beginning of their journey! Remember, it takes the average Baby Stepper two and a half to three years to knock out Baby Steps 1–3. Then it takes the average Baby Stepper about seventeen years or less to do Baby Steps 4–7 and reach a million. Think about the whole scheme of your life. That's only twenty years to reach a pinnacle point where you can have the freedom to live and give like no one else!

This is by no means a shortcut. It's just a dialed-in plan, proven by millions of ordinary people to offer the highest probability of success and the shortest distance to building wealth. The very definition of a Baby Steps Millionaire is someone who steadily, progressively works their way through the 7 Baby Steps to build a $1 million net worth or more. And if you work the plan in this way, it works every time. There's no get-rich-quick to it. But there is get-rich-faster-than-average.

Slow and Steady Wins the Race

As I shared in Chapter 1, I believe in studying successful people and emulating the habits, processes, and character traits that caused them to win. After I became a millionaire the second time and reached a net worth of $10 million, I began to wonder about billionaires. Not because I was looking to quickly jump to billionaire status overnight. I genuinely wanted to know: What habits and processes set billionaires apart? What character traits cause them to win? So, I set a goal to meet and informally interview ten billionaires in three years. I was able to do that, and to date, I have met over fifty of these rare beings! I am happy to report that all but one are some of the kindest, most generous people you could ever hope to meet. There was no arrogance or crazy behavior—they were just regular folks with a ton of money. (The "one" was an absolute nightmare, but my guess is about one out of every fifty regular people are crazy as a bean anyway, regardless of money.)

One of the first ten billionaires I met was a kind gentleman in his seventies. I had done some business with one of his companies and asked to meet with him for lunch while I was in his city doing an event. We met at a nondescript BBQ place with fabulous food. It was like having lunch with your wise uncle or grandpa—only he's a billionaire. This guy has a reputation of being a wonderful man of faith, a great family man, and very generous. Our business dealings were all calm, kind, thorough, and done with integrity. All of this gave me reason to listen to anything he had to say. That's why I really paid attention when, at the end of our conversation, he said, "Also, I have a book recommendation for you."

The prospect of this recommendation was super exciting for me because I LOVE reading books! My life has been changed by reading wonderful books. I couldn't wait to hear this billionaire's book recommendation. He must have sensed my anticipation because he strung it out with a little drama. He said, "Dave, this might be the most important book I have ever read other than the Bible. It is so important I read it to my kids and made them give me a book report on it. I have read it to every one of my grandkids, and I hope to read it to my great-grandkids before I graduate to Heaven."

Well, now I am biting down hook, line, and sinker while he reels me in. I am on the edge of that sticky chair in that fabulous BBQ restaurant, eagerly awaiting the title. "Dave, have you ever read the book, *The Tortoise and the Hare*?" he asks with a grin. I'm not going to lie. It was a bit of a letdown. Okay, maybe a major letdown. At this point I'm thinking,

You're a billionaire and an uber successful person in every area of your life, and your book recommendation is a children's fable? Ugh.

He then went on to explain that you and I live in a world of immature people who can't keep focus and are always looking for a shortcut. So, if you want to stand out, you have to learn to focus, complete tasks, and not fall for shortcuts. He concluded, "I have read that book over a thousand times, and every time I read it, the tortoise wins." *Yes, my billionaire friend—enough said.*

After our lunch meeting, I realized it had been a while since I'd read the actual Aesop's Fable, *The Tortoise and the Hare,* so I took a moment to revisit and study the old tale for myself—and then I bought the book for all of my kids and grandkids. Here it is, in case it's been a lifetime of adulting since you've read it . . .

The Tortoise and the Hare

A Hare was making fun of the Tortoise one day for being so slow.

"Do you ever get anywhere?" he asked with a mocking laugh.

"Yes," replied the Tortoise, "and I get there sooner than you think. I'll run you a race and prove it."

The Hare was much amused at the idea of running a race with the Tortoise, but for the fun of the thing he agreed. So, the Fox, who had consented to act as judge, marked the distance and started the runners off.

The Hare was soon far out of sight, and to make the Tortoise feel very deeply how ridiculous it was for him to try a race with a Hare, he lay down beside the course to take a nap until the Tortoise should catch up.

The Tortoise meanwhile kept going slowly but steadily, and, after a time, passed the place where the Hare was sleeping. But the Hare slept on very peacefully; and when at last he did wake up, the Tortoise was near the goal. The Hare now ran his swiftest, but he could not overtake the Tortoise in time.

~ The race is not always to the swift. ~

There's gold in every line! *The Tortoise and the Hare* is not just a tale to emphasize the speed at which you win but the things that get in the way of how quickly you win or that keep you from winning at all—arrogance, disrespect, idleness, neglect, poor judgment, and lack of strategy or focus. For thirty years, I've seen it over and over again. Impatient people flitting and fluttering around, laughing at those working and trusting a proven process like the Baby Steps, impulsively starting and stopping (mostly stopping like the hare), going with what feels good at the time (a nap), wanting a microwave result instead of committing to the slow simmer of the Crockpot—and then wondering why in the world they're not winning.

If this is you—if you're running the hare's race and not winning—you have to be willing to step back and honestly look at the overall picture of what has and hasn't been working. Ask yourself, *Why isn't this working? Is it arrogance or ignorance?* You need to be willing to admit you might be wrong about a few things and open to learning and trying new ways. Change can be scary, even painful, and many of you simply won't change until the pain of where you are now exceeds the pain of change. When you finally wake up and feel the full force of pain and see the results of all your get-rich-quick money decisions, you could be in your retirement years, watching all the tortoises cross the millionaire finish line ahead of you. *Or . . .* you could save yourself the trouble and change your attitude and your approach, just like Olympic skier Simen Krueger.

Simen's story is a bit of a modern-day tortoise and hare tale—with a twist. Twenty-four-year-old Simen was competing in the 2018 Winter Olympics in Pyeongchang, South Korea, representing Norway in the Men's Cross-Country Skiathlon. This was his first-ever Olympics, and Norway was known as one of the world's best ski teams. Simen was ranked seven in a field of sixty-eight skiers and was lined up to start accordingly in the front of the pack.

But just one hundred meters after the race started, Simen's right ski slipped, and he face-planted in the snow. Two rival Russian skiers directly behind him toppled right over him. It was a tangled mess of bodies, skis, and poles and about fifty other skiers navigating around them. By the time Simen was up on his skis again, he had lost thirty-six critical seconds and was dead last. "I thought it was going to be the worst day of my life with

THE QUICKEST RIGHT WAY TO A MILLION

the start I had, when I was lying on the ground with a broken pole and a ski through my bib number," he said.[39]

By race rules, Simen was able to legally replace his broken pole with a new one his coach gave him as he started back down the track. More difficult than that, though, Simen also had to replace the negative thoughts flooding into his head. At this point, he could've easily concluded there was no chance to make up the time he'd lost and just given up.[40] Instead, he chose to shift his focus and attack the 30-kilometer race first mentally, then physically. "I was last, so I had to start the race again and switch focus just to catch up with everyone," he said.[41] He coached himself to stay calm and be patient. He knew he couldn't get the seconds he'd lost back all at once, so he focused on gaining on the lead pack, steadily, lap by lap.

A skiathlon is over eighteen miles long and takes more than an hour to ski. A majority of the race is uphill. (Sounds a bit like the distance and difficulty of a millionaire's course, doesn't it?) It's hard, even when you have a normal start. But Simen kept at it. He didn't let an hour's worth of head games eat him up. He thought to himself, *Okay, take one lap, two laps, three laps, and just get into it again.* He was determined. He was diligent. And finally, he was back in contention. Then, with about three miles left, he stunned the entire world. He took the lead! Not only that, he grew his lead until he crossed the finish line—eight seconds ahead of the pack. That's right! Simen won the gold! He steadily went from a back-of-the-pack face-plant to finishing best in the world!

Simen showed us what "switch focus" means. In order to win the biggest race of his life, he needed to recalibrate from his original approach of getting to the finish the fastest. He changed his game plan to manageable steps over the long haul. He took one lap at a time and put everything he had into each lap. It took incredible focus and determination. He didn't take any shortcuts. He didn't let his foot off the gas—just steady gain after steady gain after steady gain. And it got him the gold.[42]

James Clear, author of *Atomic Habits*, says, "Patience is a competitive advantage. In a surprising number of fields, you can find success if you are willing to do the reasonable thing longer than most people." So, what's your game plan? Is it to get rich quick? If so, here's a hint from a guy who's been in a dark ballroom learning about get-rich-quick real estate schemes and went bankrupt, a guy who doesn't want to see you arrogantly fall asleep or unintentionally face-plant: It doesn't matter how you started or where you are today. Switch focus and follow the Baby Steps. They'll get you to the millionaire finish line in twenty years or less—even if there are obstacles! Along the way you'll grow your financial know-how and your strength of character so your money won't crush you but carry you forward.

I've heard the Baby Steps fable a hundred different ways, and every time I hear it, the Baby Stepper always wins.

CHAPTER 7

Will Wealth Ruin My Kids?

At eighteen years old, Ethan found himself on the brink of adulthood with more wealth than most people see in their lifetime. His dad passed away and left Ethan with $1.6 million. His parents were divorced, and his mom had been out of the picture for several years. Essentially, Ethan had loads of money and no parental guidance to count on.

At first, Ethan tried to go slow with the money and use it wisely. He took about half the money and bought a house in Lake Tahoe, remodeled it, and listed it on Airbnb. He was making about $13,000 renting it out each month, but he found himself blowing through that money faster than it could come in. His addiction was just too strong.

Ethan was spending about $10,000 a month gambling, and he just couldn't stop. Even though he had tried to get help through Gamblers Anonymous, he continued to struggle and was afraid he was going to lose everything his dad had left him if something didn't change. Desperate, he came to us.

Now, I'm no trained therapist, but I've worked with addicts on their finances for thirty years, and I've seen it time and time again: 100% of addicts end up broke if they don't heal their addiction. You name it—drug, alcohol, gambling, or sex addictions—it all has the same effect on a person's finances if left untreated. Ethan was headed down a path to destroy all of his future dreams and his dad's legacy if he didn't stop gambling. My team and I worked to help him get the financial, spiritual, and mental health resources he needed to get his life back on track and honor his dad's legacy.

Unfortunately, there are a lot of Ethans out there who are hurting and filling voids in their lives with destructive behaviors. And when money is added to the mix, it further masks the issues and amplifies the destruction. This can cause people to wonder if building wealth and leaving their children an inheritance is really a good thing after all.

The truth is, money itself is neutral and amoral. It's not good or bad. Our *behavior* is what makes money a blessing or a curse. What we *choose* to do with money is what determines its positive or negative force in our lives. There's no question that wealth is powerful, but the responsibility of it doesn't have to be heavy or harmful. With the right guidance, wealth can be helpful, even world-changing. Concerned parents often ask me, "But how? How do I keep my kids from getting messed up by money?" In this chapter, I'll show you the five specific behaviors you can model and teach your kids so money won't be a curse in their lives—or yours!

Five Behaviors to Grow Money-Smart Kids

I've checked the statistics, and I know for a fact that 100% of humans die. My wife, Sharon, and I are no exception. And that means one day, our kids are going to inherit everything we've built and saved. The same is true for you. So, this should make you pause to consider how money-smart your children really are. Will they be capable of taking care of your wealth when you're gone? Or will they struggle like Ethan? The answer to that question should fuel your motivation to teach them how to handle money the right way, right now. It could be the difference between blessing their lives beyond belief or ruining their lives beyond repair.

In our bestselling book *Smart Money Smart Kids*, my daughter Rachel Cruze and I give practical strategies on how to raise money-smart kids. Among those strategies are teaching these five simple behaviors:

- Work
- Give
- Save
- Spend
- Steward

Teaching your kids these five behaviors will help you build a strong value system to safeguard them from making bad choices with money. But fair warning: just because these principles are simple doesn't mean your children will always enjoy the learning process. I remember when my kids were teens, they each took turns complaining to Sharon and me about how "hard" it was being a Ramsey kid. They thought it was unfair that they had to manage their own checkbooks *and* work and save to buy their own cars when none of their friends had to. They thought we didn't cut them any slack.

Sharon and I aren't perfect parents by any stretch of the imagination. We did expect a lot from our kids when they were young, but we didn't do it to be mean. We wanted to make sure they understood the biblical principles of working, giving, saving, spending, and stewarding money. Because I had done stupid with money as a younger man and father, I knew firsthand how much of a curse having any amount of money could be. When I figured out it didn't have to be that way—that wealth could be a blessing, not a curse—I set out to change my family tree. That meant Sharon and I had to *intentionally decide* to shape our kids' character by these five principles and equip them with the knowledge they needed to handle money the right ways—God's ways.

Today our kids are grown, married, and have kids of their own. And they still work, give, save, spend, and steward their money. Not because Mom and Dad say so anymore, but because they internalized the principles for themselves. And it shows in the way they live and teach their kids. They work hard. They're generous. They're frugal with their saving and wise with their spending. They not only steward their wealth, but they also steward our family foundation and the business of Ramsey Solutions. Most importantly, they steward the teaching. They've taken the Baby Steps and these five principles and are now passing them on to the next generation of Ramseys. I can't tell you how proud this makes me as Papa Dave!

The thing I'm most proud of is what this means for you. It proves that the teaching works and that money doesn't ruin kids. Kids *can* learn the value of a dollar. Kids *can* develop discipline and responsibility with money. Kids *can* develop a grateful attitude that leaves no room for entitlement to take hold. And despite the horror stories the media tells us, even trust fund babies *can* manage wealth with the right guidance. So, whether you haven't started a family yet, you have a house full of kids, or your kids have left the nest, these principles—Work, Give, Save, Spend, Steward—will equip you and the next generation to win!

Work

Ben and Courtney's story is a great example of how learning the value of work and handling money at a young age can set kids up for financial success. Early on, Ben's father and grandfather taught him that if he wanted something, he needed to work and save for it instead of borrowing money to pay for it. So, he started mowing lawns when he was fourteen years old. He cut enough grass to save up and pay cash for a truck. As his business grew, he decided to increase his mowing capacity and his cash flow by saving and paying cash for a commercial grade mower. All through high school, Ben kept mowing lawns to save money for college. He was a saving machine! In fact, one of Ben's customers was a financial planner and encouraged him to open a Roth IRA. Every year since, Ben has maxed it out.

Ben went against the "normal" college experience and intentionally chose to live at home and commute to a local state university. That way, he could save on room and board and continue mowing lawns to fund his tuition. He was able to land a paid engineering internship during his junior and senior years of college. Between that internship and his lawn mowing business, Ben paid for all of his tuition and never took out a student loan. Not only that, he got a jump on homeownership. Since he avoided renting and lived at home, he was able to save up for a down payment and buy a small one-bedroom house when he was just twenty-one.

Here's a young man who got it! His family taught him the value of work, which caused him to grow his own business as a teenager and put himself through college. That's incredible! And guess what? He was really doing the Baby Steps before he was even introduced to them!

Ben first came across the Baby Steps just before his senior year in college. His church was offering *Financial Peace University* and he decided to take the class. It validated all the choices he had made to that point, and he now had a full-fledged plan to help him shape his next steps beyond college. Ben went on to graduate with an engineering degree and a new, full-time salary of $35,000 per year. Immediately he started investing 15% in the company 401(k). Two years later, he married Courtney.

They say opposites attract, but so do like-minded Baby Steppers. Ben met his wife-to-be, Courtney, during college. She was nineteen years old, working long, hard hours in fast food to pay for her tuition at a local community college. Courtney came from humble means, but her father had taught her a great work ethic. Ben admired how she wasn't materialistic and how she worked hard for what she wanted. They shared similar goals about staying out of debt and working toward financial independence. Both Ben and Courtney drove older, used cars that they paid cash for—unlike most of their friends who took out car loans. And to earn more for tuition, Courtney found a better paying job at a bank and opened a Roth IRA account as well as contributed to her 401(k). Courtney went on to graduate with an education degree and began her career as a teacher.

Once Ben and Courtney married, they started maxing out her Roth IRA. They also used the equity from Ben's first house to buy a larger two-bedroom home. They made $50,000 a year between the two of them, but they set up their budget to live off just one of their incomes so they could save and invest the rest and avoid lifestyle creep—they didn't want to spend more just because they were making more. At that point, they didn't have children, so they were focused on Baby Step 6.

Four years after graduating from college, Ben landed a much better paying job, but Ben and Courtney stayed disciplined and kept their budget locked. The extra he made allowed them to pay off their house quickly. But when their first child was born, they decided they needed more space. Because of the equity they earned with their paid-off home, they were able to build the home of their dreams—at ages thirty and twenty-seven! They made a 45% down payment and took a fifteen-year mortgage, and they paid that off in just seven years. From there, they've continued to budget with just one income. That allows them to do what they've done all along—prioritize saving and investing. It also allows them to give generously and provide great experiences for their three children.

Following the Baby Steps principles from a young age and growing their income from $50,000 to $185,000 in less than twenty years made it possible for Ben and Courtney to become millionaires before they turned forty years old. As a thirty-nine-year-old supply chain manager and a thirty-six-year-old teacher, their net worth of $1.7 million looked like this:

- $620,000 in 401(k) accounts
- $450,000 in Roth IRAs
- $230,000 in a taxable account
- $50,000 in a 529 account
- $350,000 in a paid-for house.

Neither Ben nor Courtney received any money through inheritance to get to this point. But they did inherit something much more valuable from their parents . . . the value of hard work and discipline.

Ben and Courtney's story proves that teaching kids to work and experience the reward of work can play a huge part in their future success. Mowing lawns and working fast food obviously paid off and didn't harm them in any way. Instead, it was the very foundation that helped them become millionaires before they turned forty years old! The most exciting part is that their story could really be any kid's story!

It starts with teaching our kids that work is an important life skill, just like teaching them to brush their teeth or look both ways when crossing the street. It's not child abuse, and it won't damage a kid's development or their psyche. In fact, it's a vital life skill that will play a huge part in their future success.

Allowance versus Commission

There are lots of age-appropriate ways to teach kids the value of work. First, kids need to know and understand that money comes from work. The more they work, the more they earn. It's really not rocket science, it's an emotional connection between effort and earning that many kids can grasp even at a young age. But notice how this doesn't line up with the idea of giving your child a set weekly allowance. That's because allowances are handouts. Now, I know there are a lot of well-meaning parents out there who choose to give allowances because they want their kids to have money for things. But parents commonly give allowances at the end of a week whether the chores are done or not. And it communicates to a child that even though he didn't make his bed, or she didn't rake the leaves, they will still be *allowed for* or covered regardless of their work ethic. Having a direct cause-and-effect tie between the effort and the earning builds a stronger understanding of the value of work.

Let me show you how this allowance concept plays out in the real adult world. Months after the COVID-19 pandemic hit the U.S. in 2020, there were thirty-six million people unemployed and receiving unemployment benefits. That's a big rug pulled out from under a lot of people! It reminded me of the rug pulled out from under me when I went bankrupt, except my response was to do whatever it took to get back to work. A free-market guy like myself sees this monumental unemployment mess as an unintended consequence of the federal government—both Democrats and Republicans—signing the largest stimulus bill in history. And guess what? The unemployed had no incentive to go back to work.

Instead, they experienced the debilitating effects of a handout. Handouts can seem well-meaning, but they aren't a real solution. Often the only thing they stimulate is lack of motivation, or worse, paralysis.[43] A friend of mine owns a restaurant, and once he was able to reopen after the shutdown, he had trouble staffing it because the people who used to work for him made more staying home and receiving their regular unemployment benefits *plus* $600 a week from the government.[44] In other words, they didn't have to rake the yard because they got the allowance anyway!

Putting kids on *commission* beats giving them an allowance any day. Commission honors kids' effort and causes them to feel proud of what they accomplish, not what they think they're entitled to. Earning commission gets kids motivated and excited about work and what it affords them. It gives them dignity.

When kids are young, they can start checking boxes on chore charts to visually accumulate enough completed jobs so they can buy the latest toy or video game. When they're older, they can strategize and plan out how many times they need to wash the car or mow the lawn to earn enough for the latest tech gadget or used car. Of course, pay should increase as their ages increase and the difficulty of their chores increases. But "payday" should be as consistent as possible. That said, no one is perfect. When we were in the commission stage with our kids, Sharon and I were like any other busy parents who got distracted by busy schedules, and we missed some paydays along the way. The same will be true for you. But give yourself grace. If you miss a week, just make it up as soon as you can. And remember to keep your eyes on the bigger picture. It's not about perfect execution. It's about instilling a hard-work ethic deep in the hearts of your kids.

It's important to remember, though, that not every little household chore needs to be paid for. There should be a balance between doing work for commission and doing work because your kids are simply a part of the family. Learning how to take personal responsibility, clean up after themselves, and do extra helpful things for others in the family goes a long way in setting kids up to win as future team members or leaders.

Older kids can take personal responsibility a step further. Between the ages of fourteen and eighteen, kids need to look for work opportunities outside of the home. This can be everything from starting their own babysitting or dog-walking business to taking a job scooping ice cream at the local Whippy Dip. There are a ton of important lessons that come through working with and for other people. Plus, this plants the seed that money can come from other places, not just home. And it keeps your financial safety net from becoming a hammock!

Give

What do a clenched fist and a scummy, stagnant pond have in common? Nothing can flow out of either of them!

That's a metaphor I often use to show the effects of being closed off. When fresh water can't flow in or out of a pond, it begins to stink and becomes slimy. The same is true for a person's heart—which happens to be attached to the other end of a clenched fist. If someone's heart is closed off, generosity can't flow in or out of their hands. The result is a selfish, rotten attitude. The good news is our attitudes can change. It starts by teaching our kids the second money-smart behavior after work: give.

Think about a child when he or she is asked to share their favorite toy with another child for the first time. Tears erupt. Maybe even a tug-of-war. Sharing is a tough concept. It's not a natural instinct. It requires a lot of practice to develop the skill. And that's just sharing! Giving is another level. Sharing means you still get to have a part of the thing that's shared. It means dividing something *with* someone else. Giving is transferring the ownership *to* someone else completely, usually with no expectation of getting anything in return.

Giving is an especially difficult concept for kids and adults alike. We're not born givers. We constantly battle our selfish nature and a world telling us, "It's all about me, me, me!" and, "I'm going to get—and keep—mine!" Social media only intensifies the battle. There are countless studies that show the direct tie from taking and posting selfies to a rise in self-absorbed, narcissistic behavior among Generations Y and Z. Now, I'm not saying all social media is evil. But without the right priorities, our kids can get lost in it and not realize there's a more rewarding way to live.

So how do we help our kids battle against selfishness? You guessed it—through giving. If done right, giving to others leaves no room for selfishness. When parents prioritize giving to others and actually model what that looks like for their kids, it creates an overflow effect. Kids see the impact and want to be a part of doing something good. They start to see the significance of others in relation to how they see themselves. They start to learn that they are blessed *so that* they can be a blessing.

Even when we were struggling financially, Sharon and I made a point to tithe, or give 10% of our income, to our church. Every Sunday our kids saw us put a physical envelope filled with money in the offering plate. As they got older and could understand, we shared with them how giving to the church didn't just help the church operate and serve our congregation and our community, it was also an act of spiritual obedience that honors God's generosity to us. That consistent act of giving made it easy to talk to them about how they could help too. Soon, they were putting their own money into "GIVE" envelopes.

The envelope system is a great way to teach kids how to prioritize giving and handle their money wisely. The way it works is at the end of a week, kids should divide their commission money into three envelopes: one labeled GIVE, one labeled SAVE, one labeled SPEND. We always encouraged the Ramsey kids to put 10% of their weekly earnings into their giving envelopes first, then split the rest into the other two categories. However you choose to do it, the main thing is to fund the giving envelope first to emphasize an others-first attitude, then split what's left between the other two envelopes so each envelope gets something. For simplicity's sake, keeping a stash of $1 bills around helps. So, let's say your child earned $5 that week for doing five chores at $1 per chore. They might put $1 in their giving envelope, $2 in their savings envelope, and $2 in their spending envelope. Depending on their weekly commission and their giving, saving, and spending goals, these numbers could be adjusted.

In addition to giving their money, we also taught our kids to look for ways to bless people with their time and talents. All three of our kids served on mission trips. They not only helped those less fortunate in other countries, but they also came home changed. And I'll never forget the effect the Angel Tree program had on the Ramsey kids. They bought and delivered Christmas presents to kids in the greater Nashville area who had a parent in prison. It was eye-opening for them to see firsthand the children who, without this program, would have had a present-less Christmas. I remember the looks on their faces and the change in their attitudes when they realized not everyone lived like they did. It was an important bubble-bursting moment. Giving is powerful and personal like that. It helps kids understand and appreciate their own blessings more.

Save

Once you've taught your kids to work and give, saving is next. Just like giving, saving is an essential muscle that kids—and adults—need to grow and develop. The sad reality is that, as a nation, we're really bad at saving money. A recent survey by our Ramsey Solutions Research team found that 45% of Americans have less than $1,000 saved for an emergency.[45] That means nearly half of Americans couldn't pay a single mortgage payment or buy a single month's worth of groceries for their family without putting it on a credit card or borrowing the money. Many adults have failed at saving because as children they never developed good habits to begin with. If this is true for you, the good news is you don't have to stay there. You can choose to change your family tree! You and your kids *can* learn how to save money. Personal finance is 80% behavior and 20% head knowledge. It's all about changing your behavior—replacing your bad habits with best practices. And the hardest habit to break? Impatience. So, let's start there.

We all know it—instant gratification is the name of today's game. You can check news, traffic, and weather, order breakfast and a last-minute birthday gift, and respond to seven emails all before you're done brushing your teeth. Things like apps and "easy payments" make it possible to have almost anything we want, any time we want, whether or not we have the money to pay for it.

So, if your kids see you book a family beach trip on a credit card because you and your family just "need a getaway," and then they see you freaking out about paying the bill over the next several months, that's how they'll think money works. But if they see you plan and set a goal to save and pay cash for a family vacation, they'll learn to plan, save, and pay cash for things they want too.

Planning out purchases and taking time to save for them helps you make wiser, less spontaneous decisions with your money. Delayed gratification helps you avoid buyer's remorse and months—even years—of unnecessary interest payments. Not to mention, it grows emotional maturity in us and our kids. For a younger child, saving means it will take a few *weeks* to have enough money for that special toy. For older kids, the stakes are much higher. For them, saving means it will take *months* to save for a car and a few *years* to save for that down payment on a townhouse.

Now, you've probably seen—or should I say, heard—what happens when an exhausted mom in a department store tells her five-year-old daughter she needs to wait to buy the Barbie she wants. It often results in a tantrum of epic proportions. It's like the child was given the mic for the intercom system to alert the whole store to take cover because World War III is erupting! With every scream, the other parents in the store are thinking one of two things: *Yep, I've been there and feel your pain!* or *Whew, I'm so glad that's not my kid!*

But it doesn't have to be that way. Using the commission principles and envelope system with your kids at home can eliminate drama at the store. If that same five-year-old is taught the concept of doing chores to earn and save money, then it's not world-shattering when she's told she can get the Barbie once she saves up for it. Even though she can't get the doll immediately, the girl is empowered with a plan. She knows she could go home, do some chores around the house for a couple of weeks, and then go back to the store to buy the Barbie when she's finally earned enough. She can feel proud of herself for working hard and buying that doll with money she earned herself. And mom can feel proud she didn't need cleanup in aisle 9!

The same approach can empower older kids to save for cell phones, cars, college, and any other large purchases they want or need to make. It all takes discipline and patience, but the rewards are worth it. In fact, you'll come to find it's really not about the math or the financial transactions at all. When you teach your kids to plan, set goals, and earn and save money, you're giving them tools to win at life. And before you know it, that five-year-old saving for a favorite toy will grow to be a poised, confident, and mature adult with a savings account.

Spend

As your kids learn more and more about money, they'll come face to face with a hard reality: Money has limits. It doesn't magically appear. And when it's gone, it's gone.

When she was young, our daughter Rachel ran into this reality at an amusement park. She had brought her SPEND envelope and was ready to have a full day of fun playing carnival games. But just inside the park's gate, she spotted a game where she could win a stuffed animal. Try after try, token after token, she gave it her all to win that stuffed animal until every last cent in her SPEND envelope was gone. She begged Sharon and me for more money, thinking she could pay it back later. But the answer was *No*. You can imagine how it went from there. Rachel tried her hardest, but no amount of cuteness, whining, pouting, or persuasion changed the math. As she walked around the carnival watching other kids play the games she couldn't afford to play, she realized that broke is broke. And the only way to change the outcome was to control her spending *next time*.

That might seem like a hard line to toe with a child. But I've found it's okay for the *no* to feel big to the child in the moment—big enough to change the behavior but still small enough not to scar them for life. It's better to have a hard day as a disappointed eight-year-old than to have a hard life as a forty-five-year-old chronic overspender buried under mounds of credit card debt.

That said, there's nothing "wrong" with being a spender. Sure, spenders can be impulsive, but they can also be incredibly generous. And there's nothing "right" about being a saver. Savers can tend to be more patient and responsible, but they can also be stingy. We are all wired one way or the other. The goal is to understand the personalities of our kids so we can teach them how to find the balance and be wise spenders *and* wise savers.

There are three important things that will help your child become a disciplined spender. First, your child needs to see you model wise spending. What do your spending habits look like? Are you an emotional spender? Do you find yourself buying stuff to relieve stress or get over a bad mood? These are important things to know because your kids pick up on your negative emotions and behavior, and they can get the wrong idea that buying stuff is the only way to be happy. If this is an area you struggle with, personal finance expert, my daughter, and bestselling author Rachel Cruze can help with her book *Know Yourself, Know Your Money*. She gets to the root of why you handle money the way you do so you can kick your bad spending habits for good and set a strong example for your kids.

Second, teach your kids the 24-hour rule when making purchases, especially big ones. Waiting overnight to buy something often gives a spender more clarity. The time and space away from the thing they just can't live without usually helps balance any out-of-whack emotion they're associating with the thing they want to buy on impulse. If your child wakes up the next morning and hasn't lost interest, then they should go ahead and buy it—if they can afford it!

Last, you need to teach your kids to research and gather information about their potential purchases. Encourage them to look up reviews on specific products and see what others are saying about the quality. Also, show them how to comparison shop for prices, features, and benefits so they know they're getting the best deal.

We've all made bad decisions and have done stupid with money. And as your kids learn how to spend wisely, they won't be the exception. But that's okay. Making mistakes early keeps the stakes low, but the learning high. With your correction and guidance along the way, your kids will be set up to win as wise adult spenders.

Steward

None of what I've taught you in this chapter matters unless you get this last point. You can teach your kids to work, give, save, and spend all you want. And that's a great thing—don't get me wrong! But I know I'm speaking to people who understand the possibility of becoming a millionaire. So, you already get that there's another level of wealth that can be reached. I'm talking about a special synergy that makes all of it—the working, giving, saving, spending—all come together in the way it was originally designed to. It's called stewardship. And it's what can keep us and our children from being ruined by money. I know because money almost ruined me.

As far back as I can remember, I've been driven. I set and achieved goals like I drank water. My parents helped me believe I could do anything I set my mind to if I worked hard enough. So, I set my mind to gathering "stuff." Some people call that materialism, but all I know is that I wanted me some stuff! Making money was simply a way for me to have and live the "good life," because, after all, it was all about me.

Thankfully, God got to me in my early twenties and changed me in a radical way. He called me on my self-indulgence and self-centeredness and transformed my heart into that of a giver ... and a steward. I understand that all I have is from God, so I'm going to make sure I manage it to the best of my ability and not take any of His blessings for granted.

"Steward" is an Old English word that in feudal economic times described a person who didn't own anything but only managed the affairs of the lord of the kingdom. A steward enjoyed all of the benefits of the lord's wealth. He lived in a nice house and had fine clothing and the best foods, but he had no sense of ownership over any of it. As a Christian, Jesus Christ is Lord of my life. And that changes my perspective about anything that I have. I'm simply a steward of the blessings God has given me. He is the owner. I am the manager. Do you see how that changes the focus and the significance of all the stuff you own? When you make decisions about possessions or money on behalf of someone else, it changes your attitude and behavior toward it. We're not entitled to it. We can only be grateful for it and handle it with care.

Remember Ben and Courtney? They were such good stewards of their money that they chose to live off of only one income. They took any extra money they earned and saved it or spent it wisely. As a result, they became millionaires and have the rest of their lives to bless their families and others.

If you want to raise kids who aren't selfish, let them witness a stewardship attitude in you. Let them see you manage God's resources for His glory. Let them see you work, give, save, and spend as unto the Lord (Colossians 3:23). If you want kids to view wealth as a responsibility, not an excuse to buy whatever they want, teach them how to steward what they have.

Putting It All Together

Some of you will read this chapter and feel like it's impossible to teach your kids these things. You need to remember it's not an overnight process. God didn't design it so our kids would come out of the womb as adults, and we'd have minutes to teach them everything they need to know to be functioning and wise before we release them into the real world. He gave us infants to raise and grow over the course of nearly twenty years. And even then, the teaching doesn't need to stop! But it does need to start.

There's no such thing as a perfect parent. Despite all of our imperfections and money mistakes, we still have a choice to keep trying. We still have a choice to do right by our kids and set them up to win. I was the dad who went bankrupt, remember? But I was also the dad who decided to change my family tree and do better for my kids and grandkids. I was the dad who stayed in the game and didn't give up. That's how I know you can do this too!

Regardless of your past financial failings, there is always hope. You *can* teach your kids to be money-smart. These five behaviors will give you the framework. Teaching your kids to work, give, save, spend, and steward will be a safeguard against entitlement, selfishness, stinginess, overindulgence, and waywardness. Most of all, this framework will be the foundation of your legacy. With these skills, your kids feel prepared and capable to take on the responsibility of managing their wealth and yours for generations to come. That's a life changer!

Deuteronomy 30:19 tells us, "I call heaven and earth as witnesses today against you, that I have set before you life and death, blessing and cursing; therefore choose life, that both you and your descendants may live" (NKJV). I think about the Ethans of the world and my heart breaks. And then I think about the Bens and Courtneys of the world and I know the story line can be different. As parents, we have a choice to get this right. I guarantee it won't be perfect, but make a commitment and put your focus where it matters most. Choose life and a legacy of blessing for your children. You can do this!

CHAPTER 8

Wealth and the Wealthy Are NOT Evil

Big, white clouds of steam rolled out from under the hood of my car—the latest in a long line of noble, terribly unreliable junkers I drove after Sharon and I went broke. I was on my way to a speaking event with one of my VPs, and now we were stranded in a gas station parking lot watching my car have a spectacular meltdown—and I was angry. Not about my car overheating. I was angry at myself.

The fact was it was past time for me to get a new car. It's true, the last ten years had been hard. Sharon and I had worked like crazy to get out of debt and pay off the bankruptcy. We fought our way out of that mess by following biblical principles, and God had blessed us. By this time, we were building wealth again and our net worth was over a million dollars. The money was in the bank for me to get a nicer car. But I was used to driving junkers. And honestly, I was focused on more important things than buying a new car. But my VP didn't let me off the hook. As we dug through the trash for a jug we could use to pour water into the radiator to cool it down, he pointed out the ridiculousness of our situation: "You seriously have to get a better car. This is crazy! You have the money."

There was no point in arguing. He was absolutely right, and I knew it. So, I shopped around until I found a great deal on a two-year-old Jaguar. It was sweet! I drove a Jag right before I went broke, and that made this car even more special. The first day I drove it to my office building, I took a minute to just admire my "new" car as it gleamed in the sunlight. The moment couldn't have been more perfect. After all, I'd done things *right* this time. I paid cash for that car, and it was a completely reasonable purchase for my family. To me, it was a physical symbol that God's ways of handling money actually work—that I could build wealth the right way. But that's not what I was thinking about. Standing there in that parking lot with my beautiful car, I was suddenly questioning my decision: *Did I do something wrong?*

The problem with the Baby Steps is that they actually work. If you do the things we teach, you *will* build wealth. And the last thing I want is for you to end up standing right where I was, on your way to becoming a Baby Steps Millionaire and feeling some weird sense of guilt about your wealth.

I didn't do anything wrong when I bought that car. In fact, I believe God smiled at me when I wrote the check. Trust me, I know how shocking that sounds. That's because we're surrounded by loud voices in our culture today who constantly beat the drum that wealth is bad. You know what I'm talking about because you see it every day, and it can be hard not to buy into the arguments. Tell me if you've heard this before: "No Christian should ever own such an expensive car!" Or, "The rich keep getting richer, and the poor keep getting poorer!" How about, "The system is rigged against the little man—only big business can win these days."

The message is clear, isn't it? Wealth isn't just bad—it's evil. *Only greedy, rich people have money. Wealthy Christians (if it's possible to be wealthy and Christian) should give all their money away! Don't you know the only way for someone to become wealthy is to take advantage of others? It's just not right for some people to have so much while others have so little!*

Don't buy into any of that! These toxic, misguided ideas about wealth have seeped into church, politics, and government, and they have the potential to wreck our future as a society. You need to be ready for the unhealthy messages you'll have to deal with—if you aren't already—as you become a Baby Steps Millionaire. And honestly, when you know the truth, it's easy to see where these anti-wealth arguments fall apart.

Equal Is Not Fair

First, let's dig into the idea that wealth ought to be equal. Occasionally, folks call into my show to argue with me about this topic. The interesting thing is, they agree with me on just about everything else—that people need to budget, live below their means, and plan for the future. But they disagree wholeheartedly when I say wealth and income inequality is a good thing. Isn't that strange? As I listen to their arguments, however, I've noticed they're never based on facts. "The gap between the rich and the poor is getting wider and wider! That's just not right," they'll say. Or, "The 'system' is rigged in favor of the rich and 'big business.' It's unfair!" There's a lot of emotion in what they're saying, but very little fact. And that's not truly shocking. After all, they hear the same messages I do that "greedy rich people" are what's wrong with the world. And we all know that's *not* based in fact.

What's really happening is that those folks are operating with a scarcity mindset. A scarcity mindset says there's only so much wealth to go around. And because I have more than you do, I've taken away your opportunity to have more. They're picturing it like a pie, and they're fighting to get what's left after the "greedy rich people" have taken a huge piece for themselves. They believe that for the world to be fair, wealth and income must be equal.

Well, here's a fact for you: Unequal is more fair than equal. Or, to put it another way, equal is *unfair*. Why? Because effort is not equal. Talent is not equal. Intelligence is not equal. Here's a different kind of example: If one college student goofs off in class, doesn't do his homework, and makes an F on the test, should he get an A in the class just like the student who pays attention, turns in his homework, and aces the test? Of course not. That would be unfair. There was a different level of effort and a different level of intelligence. The results should not be equal.

The same thing goes for wealth. It would be unfair if we all had equal income or wealth.[46] That's because we don't all bring the same level of economic service to the marketplace. That's not the same thing as your value as a human being. You have great value as a human being, and we all have equal value before God. But don't confuse your value as a human with the value you bring to the marketplace. Your pay is not a reflection of your value as a person, and it shouldn't be. Your pay is a reflection of the service you bring to the marketplace—and that's what generates wealth.

The restaurant owner who runs his business well serves the marketplace in a larger capacity than the host or cook or dishwasher who works there. So, the owner's income is higher. If he opens more restaurants, hires more employees, and serves the marketplace at an even greater capacity, his income should reflect that.

Now, if you're Guy Fieri, a celebrity chef who also hosts *Diners, Drive-Ins, and Dives* and *Guy's Grocery Games* on the Food Network, your value in the marketplace is in another league altogether. I don't normally pay attention to what goes on at the Food Network. But when Guy recently landed an $80 million contract to renew his two shows and give him a $50 million raise, I noticed. I mean, that's professional athlete-level wealth, isn't it?

A lot of people see that and get a chip on their shoulder: "No one is worth that kind of money! How can anyone get paid $80 million to host a TV show about food?" Well, why shouldn't Guy get paid $80 million? He's not getting paid $80 million because he's a better human being than you or me. He's getting paid $80 million because he's a better TV show host than you or me, and because it's a good deal for his employer. According to *Forbes*, Guy's shows generated more than $230 million in revenue in 2020 for the Food Network. I think Guy's contract is going to work out pretty well for them, too, don't you?[47]

Most of us who've lived a little life already know the concept of wealth equality is completely *unfair*. And that's not a feeling I have—it's a fact. In a 1978 survey, Americans under age thirty were the most likely of any age group (54%) to support wealth redistribution with the goal to achieve wealth equality through higher taxes on the rich. Almost thirty years later, a similar study showed a drastic change in their views. In the new study, the majority (65–71%) of people who would have been roughly age thirty at the time of the 1978 study now said they *oppose* higher taxes and wealth redistribution.[48] It doesn't take a genius to figure out why. As people get older and start working and paying taxes, they realize the government will target *their* wealth to give away. Everyone's a philosopher until they start writing the checks, right? Sounds like those good-hearted young folks turned into some old, greedy rich people, doesn't it? Or maybe they just realized what you already know—that no government program has the power to truly change your financial situation for the better. It's up to you. And with enough hard work and discipline, *anyone* can take control of their financial future and become a millionaire.

The Truth about Wealth

The anti-wealth crowd can demonize "greedy rich people" and clamor for wealth equality all they want, but that doesn't change one important fact. The ultimate flaw in the "wealth is bad" ideology is this: If you're reading this book and you live in North America, you're rich. That's not an exaggeration. It's just the truth.

The average household income in America is more than $65,000.[49] But let's say your family is well below the U.S. average, and your household income is $29,000 a year. That actually puts you in the top 5% of income earners in the world.[50] No kidding. After taxes, you're bringing home right around $2,000 a month, but you're earning more than 95% of the rest of the global population. Let's take it a step further. Let's say your household income is $10,500—well below minimum wage in the U.S. You're still in the top 20% of income earners in the world.[51] You're better off, income-wise, than eight in ten people worldwide.

Listen, if you're making $10,500, $29,000, or even $65,000, I know you probably don't feel rich. That's because we compare ourselves to other Americans who we think are better off than we are. But globally speaking, America has some of the richest poor people on earth. If you don't believe me, all you have to do is visit a country where the average person lives in a shack with no running water. Many don't know where their next meal is coming from. Then you come home to running water, indoor plumbing, and food in the pantry, and it doesn't take long to realize how wealthy you really are.

Can you see how this one fact flattens the "wealth is bad" belief system? It doesn't make sense that $29,000 is a "humble" or "righteous" amount of money in the U.S. *and* an "evil" or "greedy" amount of wealth globally at the same time. How can any of us shame those greedy rich people when we are all, from a global perspective, rich people ourselves?

A good friend of mine, Rabbi Daniel Lapin, is an orthodox Jewish rabbi, and he's taught me a lot about the way the Jewish culture views money and wealth. Why would an evangelical Christian like me be interested in what Jewish people believe about wealth? Well, as Rabbi Lapin explains in his book *Thou Shalt Prosper*, Jewish people, who are a minority in America, consistently have a disproportionate amount of wealth.

A demographic study of the Forbes 400, the richest people in America, showed thirty Jewish people made the top one hundred on the list.[52] If Jewish folks represent 30% of the richest people in America but make up only 2% of the U.S. population, I think that's worth digging into, don't you? Rabbi Lapin's book lays out "Ten Commandments for Making Money" according to Jewish tradition. The first and most important is that Jewish tradition views a person's quest for profit and wealth to be inherently moral.

Don't miss that! "Inherently moral" is the opposite of evil. And the Bible makes this connection for Christians, too, in 1 Timothy 5:8: "But if anyone does not provide for his own, and especially for those of his household, he has denied the faith and is worse than an unbeliever" (NKJV). In order to provide for the needs of your family, you have to make money, and few people will argue with the morality of that. But Rabbi Lapin says Jewish tradition doesn't stop there.

The *Havdalah* is an ancient ceremony Jewish families perform to prepare for the coming work week. It's recited over a cup of wine that runs over into a saucer and symbolizes their wealth, among other things, and how they intend to use it. First, they fill the cup, providing for their own needs. Then they keep pouring until the cup overflows and they have plenty to give to others. I love this image so much I've used it in my live events and video classes. It's such a beautiful illustration of how we should view our wealth and our reasons for wealth building.

In Chapter 4, we talked about how important your beliefs are to your success in becoming a Baby Steps Millionaire. The Jewish cultural belief that making money is a moral act has likely had the most influence on Jewish success in business. It's how they've been able to prosper no matter where they are. The fastest way to undermine your or anyone else's chances of success is to say that making money is selfish, greedy, or evil. Only a self-serving jerk would pursue success if that were true, right? But that's exactly what our culture says. Wealth is bad. Wealthy people are evil and greedy. It's why I second-guessed my decision to buy my new car. Don't fall into that trap! Your pursuit of wealth and success is moral—as long as you do it with an unselfish, not greedy, biblical perspective.

King Solomon was the richest person in the world—at least up until his time. He was also one of the wisest people ever to live. That didn't keep him from making some mistakes and learning a lot of lessons the hard way. And even though he had personal experiences with many of the pitfalls of wealth, Solomon says this in the Bible:

> Here is what I have seen: It is good and fitting for one to eat and drink, and to enjoy the good of all his labor in which he toils under the sun all the days of his life which God gives him; for it is his heritage. As for every man to whom God has given riches and wealth, and given him power to eat of it, to receive his heritage and rejoice in his labor—this is the gift of God. (Ecclesiastes 5:18–19, NKJV)

So, the Bible says God gives riches and wealth and gives man the power to eat of it and to rejoice in his labor. Sounds pretty clear to me. Not only is building wealth okay—it's even okay to *enjoy* wealth. Again, it all has to do with your attitude about money. If you keep your perspective straight and never forget that you are just a manager of what God owns, then, yes, you have the right to enjoy the blessings and benefits of the wealth He entrusts to you.

Toxic Views of Wealth in the Church

I imagine a lot of Christian readers are struggling to take in that message right now—that God is more than okay with us building and enjoying wealth—that it's actually our *heritage*! That's because toxic views of wealth often show up in the church as well. As a Christian who's made money teaching biblical financial principles, I've heard every supposedly Bible-based argument against wealth you can think of—from believers and nonbelievers. The problem is those folks have built their reasoning on nothing more than misunderstandings and misinterpretations of scripture.

Here's a classic: Money is the root of all evil. Wrong! Money is *not* the root of all evil. The Bible does *not* say that, no matter how many times you've heard it. Here's what 1 Timothy 6:10 actually says: "For the *love* of money is *a* root of *all kinds* of evil" (NKJV, emphasis added). Money isn't the problem. The love of money is the problem.

Listen, money—by itself—isn't good or bad. It's an inanimate object, just like the coffee table in your living room. It's just a table. It's just money. But what people do with and for money can be good or evil. The people at St. Jude's Hospital do a lot of good with money. On the other hand, drug cartels in South America do a lot of evil with and for money. The bottom line behind 1 Timothy 6:10 is that God doesn't like it when we worship anything other than Him. We worship the Provider, not the provision. If money—or anything else—gets in the way of our relationship with Him, then we have a problem. He doesn't like that.

Here's another anti-wealth sentiment: "Have you not heard, Dave, that rich people aren't going to heaven? It says it right here. It's easier for a camel to go through the eye of a needle than for a rich man to enter the kingdom of God (Luke 18:25)! Your wealth is going to send you straight to hell!" People have preached that message at me a thousand times—these days mostly on social media—and they usually don't know any other verse in the whole Bible. The sad thing is, they have no idea what that passage is all about. In fact, I believe Luke 18:18–27 may be one of the most misinterpreted passages in the whole Bible, so let's take a look at what it *really* says:

Now a certain ruler asked Him, saying, "Good Teacher, what shall I do to inherit eternal life?" So, Jesus said to him, "Why do you call Me good? No one is good but One, that is, God. You know the commandments: 'Do not commit adultery,' 'Do not murder,' 'Do not steal,' 'Do not bear false witness,' 'Honor your father and your mother.'" And he said, "All these things I have kept from my youth." So, when Jesus heard these things, He said to him, "You still lack one thing. Sell all that you have and distribute to the poor, and you will have treasure in heaven; and come, follow Me." But when he heard this, he became very sorrowful, for he was very rich. And when Jesus saw that he became very sorrowful, He said, "How hard it is for those who have riches to enter the kingdom of God! For it is easier for a camel to go through the eye of a needle than for a rich man to enter the kingdom of God." (Luke 18:18–25, NKJV)

According to the anti-wealth crowd, this is all the proof you need that rich people are barred from an eternity in heaven. According to this crowd, North American reader, you should prepare for hell, because globally, you're rich. Ridiculous! And sure, if you just read these verses by themselves, without the context of the story or the greater teaching, you can reach the logical conclusion that wealth is evil. There was no other reason for this guy not to make it to heaven. He'd done everything the Law required. Then, Jesus told him to do one more thing—sell everything he owned.

But Jesus is looking right into this guy's heart. This guy was following a legal checklist, thinking it would get him into heaven because he was of the religious elite. But checking off boxes isn't going to get you to heaven. Neither is a bunch of money, for that matter. And this guy's wealth had become a stumbling block between him and God. When the young, rich guy walked away sad, Jesus makes a comment that sounds like a condemnation against all wealth: "How hard it is for those who have riches to enter the kingdom of God! For it is easier for a camel to go through the eye of a needle than for a rich man to enter the kingdom of God" (Luke 18:24–25, NKJV).

And that's where most people stop reading. They say, "Well there it is, Dave. It couldn't be clearer!" But you've got to keep reading! The true heart of the passage is found in the next two verses. Jesus's comment in verse 25 shocks the crowd who had just witnessed the conversation between Jesus and the rich guy. So, they ask, "Who then can be saved?" (v. 26). In those days, people believed wealth was a one-way ticket to heaven. Many thought that you could buy your way into heaven, while others saw wealth as a sure sign of God's favor. And here's Jesus, blowing their minds by saying how hard it is for the rich to enter the kingdom of God. What chance did they have to get to heaven if you can't get there by following the Law or becoming rich? That one bit of context changes the whole passage, doesn't it? It's not a condemnation of wealth. It's a desperate plea for help.

Jesus immediately answers their question (and hang on, because now He's going to blow *your* mind!). He says, "The things which are impossible with men are possible with God" (Luke 18:27, NKJV). Surprise! This passage isn't about whether rich people can get to heaven or not. Jesus is not teaching us that you must give everything away to get into heaven. In fact, there's no doctrine about money here at all.

Jesus is giving us a powerful teaching about grace. There's only one way to heaven, and that's through Jesus Christ. Salvation was impossible for the rich ruler and it's impossible for you and me—not because of our wealth or lack of it. It's impossible because we are all sinners. None of us—rich or poor, drug addict or murderer, gossip or prostitute— none of us can get to heaven on our own. Our salvation is entirely in God's hands, and He alone makes the impossible possible. Using this scripture to say rich people can't go to heaven is absurd and doctrinally broken.

If you want to know the truth, the idea that the doors of heaven are closed to the rich because of their wealth is actually a form of heresy called Gnosticism. When someone says those doors are closed, they're essentially saying that Jesus's sacrifice on the cross is not enough to provide salvation to someone who has too many zeros on their balance sheet. And that, my friends, is just a load of heresy.

What's It All For?

We've just talked a lot about the world's toxic views of wealth. I hope you know that wealth isn't a barrier to communing with God or getting into heaven. I hope you understand that wealth isn't evil; it's amoral. Instead, it's what you do with your wealth that matters.

That brings us to the question: Why do we ultimately build wealth? What drives us to put in the effort, make the sacrifices, and risk being misunderstood by our friends and family along the way? For security—sure. To change our future and our family's future for generations to come? Of course! But wealth building is about more than me and mine. It's also about making a difference in our communities and in the world through our giving. Generosity is a hallmark character quality of those who win with money. Seven in ten millionaires in our study say they set money aside each month to give to others. But it's tough to get any of them to talk about it!

Let me tell you about Steve—because you'll never hear this story from Steve himself. Steve is a member of a very cool, very expensive country club I visited once to play golf.

I went with a friend—and my friend knew a guy who got me in. It's *that* exclusive. Not a blade of grass is out of place. It's where the upper crust—the super-rich—hang out. Normally, I feel like a wiener in a steakhouse in a place like this, but this day I belonged. The guys I met there aren't from old money. Like me and 90% of the millionaires in our study, they're first-generation rich. They hadn't inherited a dime.

While I was there, I got to know Miguel, a golf attendant who met me at the door with a huge smile on his face. He couldn't wait to serve me. He told me he listens to me on the radio and would be honored to care for me during my day with him. My new friends from the golf course said Miguel is always like that—smiling, caring, serving. He takes pride in his work, and you can tell. Miguel and I snapped a picture together, and I was honored to do it. Later, after a few hours of golf, my new golf buddies and I sat on the deck overlooking the course, and out pops Miguel. He hands me our picture from that morning and wants me to sign it. Of course I sign it—again it's an honor for me.

After Miguel leaves, one of my new friends tells us Miguel is about to graduate with his master's degree in engineering. Man—I was already a Miguel fan. And I'm loving him more every minute! But that's not all. My new friend shares with our small group that Steve, a friend of my friend I never got to meet, is paying Miguel's tuition. None of the other guys in the group—some of them close friends of Steve—had any idea he was paying for Miguel's schooling. But we all smile because we understand. Steve didn't do it to show off or to win some Generosity Award. First-generation millionaires—Baby Steps Millionaires—are some of the most generous people you'll ever meet. But you'll never know this side of heaven just how generous they are—because they don't do it for the attention.

Before I left, I talked with Miguel again. He trotted out to save me from the hassle of having to carry my own bag to my car. I told you—Miguel is a prize! I shared with him that I'd heard he was getting his master's in engineering. And if it's possible, he lit up even more, and I think I saw his chest stick out a little as he said, "I came to this country with nothing in my backpack but dreams. Someday I will belong to a club like this." I have no doubt that Miguel will do exactly that. And when he does, he will be compelled by the unwritten playbook of generosity like his friend Steve. And he will pay it forward to give someone else like him a shot.

Steve is not alone in making a big, but quiet, difference in the lives of the people around him. Baby Steps Millionaires all over the country are finding simple, everyday ways to show their generosity. We had to dig deep into our social media pages to find their stories because Baby Steps Millionaires don't brag about their giving. We found a post from Cheryl who told us how she accepted the "tip the bill challenge," where people tip their restaurant servers 100% of the bill. She tipped 100% on a $125 bill—gifting her server $125 and making her night!

Susan shared a story similar to many others. She told us, "The lady in front of me at the grocery store was digging in her bag and couldn't find her money to pay her bill. I silently caught the attention of the check-out lady, slid her my debit card, and she very discreetly finished the lady's transaction. She gave the lady her receipt and, with a smile, said, 'There you go, ma'am. You're all set.' I had no idea how much the lady's tab was. But it didn't matter because I knew I had enough in my account to cover it."

Baby Steps Millionaires have told us how they've paid school tuition for a friend—anonymously. Or that they're the "matching donor" for charity fundraisers in their community. Or that they provide support for a small, rural school. They're donating used vehicles to families in need and buying Christmas gifts for thirty kids at a time!

Stories like this remind me of these healthy shakes my wife drinks. Sharon is a runner, does yoga, plays golf—she's in great shape, and she makes me a little sick. Lately though, she's been blending up things that were not meant by God to go into a shake, healthy or otherwise. Brussels sprouts and broccoli—I mean, you can just imagine what that looks like in a glass, right? It's gross, green and slimy, and when I look at it, I think I'd just rather go hungry. One day, she blended up one of these things and left some in the bottom of the glass. Then she set it in the sink, turned the faucet on and walked away for a second. Now, picture this with me for a minute. As the clean water pours into that filthy, dirty glass, all the disgusting green stuff starts bubbling out. As more clean water goes in, it displaces all the nasty brussels sprouts, until finally, you have a glass of sparkling clean water. The bad stuff is gone because the clean stuff displaced it.

That's what Baby Steps Millionaires can and are doing with their money through giving. Evil doesn't pay for people's groceries or gift people college tuition or donate used cars. The more Baby Steps Millionaires we have doing these kinds of things, the better our society will be. That's the whole point of building wealth with the Baby Steps! Not for ourselves. Not for our glory or to satisfy our human love of stuff. We build wealth by following biblical principles and in turn, manage it for God's Kingdom to help others. Through us, God can show up right when people need it the most. What could possibly be evil about that? That's right. Nothing!

CHAPTER 9

Baby Steps Millionaires in Every Neighborhood

What did your neighborhood look like growing up? My neighborhood was just outside of Nashville, Tennessee, in a town called Antioch. In the '60s, Antioch was far from what we consider "the 'burbs" now, but I guess because of its location, you could've called it that. It was more rural than city at that time and definitely didn't have the wealth of a typical city suburb as we know it today.

As a boy, I wasn't too concerned about those kinds of things. I was too busy cutting through neighbors' yards with all my hillbilly friends, playing whatever the game of the day was—sometimes football in whichever yard you could go for the longest touchdown pass, sometimes hockey in the street. From after breakfast until we heard our moms call us for lunch, we'd run without a care in the world. And then we'd get right back at it and run until it was dark and we couldn't see who was on the other end of the touchdown pass.

Where I grew up was a far cry from my friend Rafael's neighborhood in El Salvador. In his neighborhood, people were running for much more serious reasons. In the 1980s, El Salvador was at the beginning of a civil war—a war that would last more than a decade and end with tens of thousands dead and even more living in horrifying conditions and without food or clean water. The *New York Times* described it like this:

> The five million people of this Massachusetts-sized nation are jammed into a narrow, mountainous corridor hard to find on a map . . . the per-capita income is less than $700, one of the lowest in the Western hemisphere. . . .
>
> Malnutrition is endemic in El Salvador . . . Functional illiteracy among the peasants approaches 95 percent.
>
> And some 60 percent of El Salvador's population is rural, living in isolated valleys or mountain hamlets. . . . Hundreds of thousands of peasants live in hovels made of packed mud; naked children with swollen bellies and open sores wander among the grunting pigs, garbage and flies. Their mothers and sisters trudge for an hour or more to the nearest well for water. . . ."[53]

Rafael was born the fifth of seven children, and he and his parents and siblings all lived in war-torn El Salvador with his grandparents. It goes without saying he was born into poverty. But though his family was poor, Rafael said he learned to cherish the little things. His grandparents taught him farm work and the value of family. You can imagine then why, when Rafael was about four years old, his mom and dad made the difficult decision to leave him and his siblings with his grandparents in El Salvador and travel to the United States in search of work and a better way of life for their kids.

The couple landed in the farming community of Grandview, Washington, among a large population of other migrant and immigrant workers. Three years later, seven-year-old Rafael and his siblings were reunited with them there. While the situation was better, it wasn't great. They basically exchanged third-world poverty for first-world poverty, but poverty nonetheless.

For Rafael and his siblings, poverty was the only thing they'd ever known. In Grandview, they lived on welfare and in subsidized housing with lots of government assistance, including free school lunches. But it was still an upgrade compared to El Salvador. As a result, Rafael learned how to be frugal with money. He said, "When there are seven mouths to feed and your parents are working for minimum wage, you learn to cherish that one pair of tennis shoes or that new pair of jeans from Walmart. Frugality gets instilled into you."

After high school, the U.S. Army gave Rafael a way to pursue an affordable career track. Plus, it helped him continue to pursue physical fitness, something he'd been passionate about since he was a boy. It was also through the Army that Rafael met his wife, JoBeth. On his first tour of duty, he was stationed in Hawaii. JoBeth's dad was an Army officer who also happened to be stationed in Hawaii. It wasn't long before twenty-one-year-old Rafael married eighteen-year-old JoBeth, and they started their life together.

As most couples do, they learned the hard way that they didn't have the same ways of handling money. While Rafael's family had taught him how to make every penny count, JoBeth's family handled money differently. Her dad was the primary breadwinner and was often away from home on deployment. Her mom was more of a free spirit when it came to spending money, but did her best to handle the household, raise the kids, and manage the finances when her husband wasn't around to serve as an accountability partner. Penny pinching wasn't always the priority.

It's no surprise then, that Rafael and JoBeth's different financial backgrounds translated into having some debt early in their marriage. Four years in, they bought their first house and then took out a $20,000 HELOC (home equity line of credit) against it to buy furniture, appliances, and other "necessities" for a new home. They also had car loans and three credit cards that they tried to pay off every month. But it wasn't long before the balances carried over from month-to-month and interest started racking up—the good ol' American Way. This is how it went for about ten years until they involuntarily discovered *Financial Peace University*.

After the Army, Rafael transitioned to a role in federal law enforcement. He was transferred to a training center where, among Rafael's other duties, his supervisor wanted him to lead the military version of *Financial Peace University*. This is a special version of *Financial Peace University*, uniquely designed for military families who rank financial stress as the number one stressor of military life, even over active-duty relocation.[54] Even though Rafael was interested in training others in all forms of fitness and personal development, he really didn't have any interest in leading *Financial Peace University* because he didn't know much about the program or "that Dave Ramsey guy." But he didn't have a choice. His director instructed him to lead it, so he had to, whether he liked it or not. Thankfully, the more Rafael taught the program, the more he realized it was an effective approach to financial fitness.

Over time, the Baby Steps in *Financial Peace University* really resonated with Rafael. He and JoBeth had already set aside money in emergency savings, and they didn't have car loans anymore. Even so, they realized that they were only doing about 75–80% of the Baby Steps (we call this "Ramsey-ish"), and they pinpointed some areas where they still needed to get on board. They decided to go all in and really focus on handling money with the same intensity they had always given to their physical well-being and other areas of their personal development. They started budgeting together, cut up their last remaining credit card, and haven't looked back! For the first time, they began following the Baby Steps exactly. In Baby Step 2, they got rid of all debt for good, then finished their emergency fund in Baby Step 3. They began investing 15% into their retirement with a nice match for Baby Step 4.

Fast-forward six years. Rafael is now forty years old, JoBeth is thirty-seven, and because they followed the Baby Steps, their life is on a completely new trajectory. They paid off their home early, knocking out Baby Step 6. And with that equity added to their savings and retirement accounts, they reached a $1.1 million net worth. It breaks down like this:

- $700,000 in their TSP (Thrift Savings Plan)
- $300,000 in equity in their paid-for home
- $30,000 in two Roth IRAs
- $30,000 in savings
- $40,000 in other assets.

Now, sixteen years from that first Baby Step, Rafael and JoBeth are on Baby Step 7 and have their sights set on retiring in their early fifties. Remember, during that sixteen years, they were not perfect. Early on, they weren't 100% on board with the plan. But they learned and grew and finally worked the Baby Steps properly. They plan to continue to build wealth and optimize the next ten years by maxing out each of their Roth accounts and getting their 5% match. Their financial advisor conservatively projects a $2.9 million portfolio in ten years at an 11% ROI. This, plus their full pension benefits, will make for a really nice retirement, don't you think?

Rafael and JoBeth built their wealth by working hard and investing early. They didn't attend college and never received any sort of inheritance or leveraged any debt to hit the millionaire mark. In their first year of marriage, they earned only $20,000 on Rafael's Army salary, while the Army covered their housing and other living expenses. Since then, JoBeth started working in federal law enforcement doing administrative and human resources work. Nineteen years later, they've grown their combined income to around $200,000.

Rafael and JoBeth are heroes! And not just because they followed the Baby Steps and grew a $1.1 million net worth. They are heroes because they worked the poverty mindset out of their hearts. (My friend who grew up in "the 'hood" says it's easier to get out of the 'hood than to get the 'hood out of your heart.)

But most importantly, Rafael and JoBeth are heroes because of what they're doing to help others. They have lived like no one else, so they can live and give like no one else now.

The couple gives generously to their church and to charities. "Giving . . . is a heart thing," said Rafael. "We found a great church and we began to faithfully trust our finances to God. We started to give Him our first fruits—our tithe. It's amazing to us how initially the tithe didn't even seem to fit into our spreadsheet, and yet God multiplied our provision and has given us more blessings than we have room for."

On top of their monetary giving, they've also given their time and led multiple *Financial Peace University* classes together. One of the most exciting classes they've led included JoBeth's parents. "They said they would take the class, but they weren't going to cut up any credit cards," Rafael explained. "By the third week, they were cutting up their credit cards!" How about that? Rafael and JoBeth are impacting people in their neighborhood *and* changing their family tree!

Not only that, but remember the guy who *involuntarily* had to lead *Financial Peace University*? Well, now Rafael's a financial coach! In addition to his law enforcement work, he's gone through Ramsey's *Financial Coach Master Training* and serves his clients with the same Baby Steps principles that helped him and JoBeth become millionaires.

Rafael was twenty-five when he started investing in his TSP account. When asked what advice he would give to a twenty-five-year-old, he said he would tell them what he has told his coaching clients and his three children: "First, *it is possible* to become a millionaire today. We're examples of that. Continue your self-development and personal development. Attend *Financial Peace University* to improve your financial IQ. A dollar invested in your twenties has the ability to multiply itself over and over. The key is time in the market, not timing the market." I couldn't have said it better myself!

So, let's pause here and really take in Rafael and JoBeth's story. Rafael was born outside of America in stark poverty. Then he immigrated to America and again lived in poverty. He's a first-generation American citizen who served in the U.S. military. He and JoBeth married young and, like most of us, made mistakes with money. Then they discovered the Baby Steps and learned how to handle money the right way. They grew their income from $20,000 to $200,000 and became millionaires by the age of forty. It took them sixteen years total, one year less than the time it takes an average Baby Steps Millionaire to complete Baby Steps 4–7. They plan to retire early at age fifty with a $2.9 million portfolio. And all along the way, they've continued to spread the millionaire message to their family, friends, and community. Wow! This is what it's all about!

The Baby Steps Are for Everyone

You know what I see in Rafael and JoBeth's story and the handful of other millionaires' stories throughout this book—Tiffany, John and Maddi, Webster, Clint and Brittany, Melanie and JD, Jackie, Ben and Courtney? Every man. Every woman. Every ethnicity. Every creed. Every age. Every marital status. Every learning style. Every career. Every neighborhood in every region of the country. Every freaking starting point! Every person who never dreamed of being a millionaire . . . but then realized it was possible.

After reading their stories and the mind-blowing statistics peppered throughout these pages, the bigger question is: **What do YOU believe is possible for YOU?** Your answer is what all of this comes down to. Can you follow Baby Steps 1–7? Absolutely! But will you? Can you get past what the world tells you is possible or impossible? Yes, but will you? Can you become a millionaire? Yes, without a doubt. But will you?

How Big Is Your Hope?

John Johnson, founder of *Ebony* magazine said, "Men and women are limited not by their intelligence, nor by their education, not by the color of their skin, but by the size of their hope."

Maybe when you started reading this book, your hope was small, minimized or stolen by past failures or lost perspective. Or maybe you just put your hope in the wrong things. Maybe you believed or said things like:

People like me never win.

I flunked that math class, so I'll never be good at finances.

I invested once, and it didn't work, so I don't invest.

I've done stupid with money, and I don't deserve to be wealthy.

The amazing thing is that if we can have the right perspective on our circumstances and obstacles and learn from our past mistakes and failures, they can actually be an indicator of our future success and our reason for hope.

When Tiffany found herself single and raising two kids on a small salary, she didn't just give up. Instead, she did what she could, little by little, until she could grow her margin enough to reach the millionaire mark. When John and Maddi teetered on the brink of divorce, they dug in and refused to let money fights rob them of financial peace. When Webster fully realized he had a learning disability, it gave him a chance to understand its complexities and become educated and wealthy in spite of it. When Clint and Brittany, Melanie and JD, and Ben and Courtney all calculated a "normal" life saddled with student loan debt, they made the less popular choice to follow a different plan than their friends—and all became millionaires before the age of forty. And when Jackie and Rafael and JoBeth recognized the curse of poverty and systemic barriers in their lives, they were able to break the chains with the Baby Steps, build wealth, and change their family trees.

As they all gained perspective and took control of their situations, they grew their hope. Proverbs 13:12 says, "Hope deferred makes the heart sick, but when the desire comes, it is a tree of life" (NKJV). Without hope, we're not well. But with hope, we can have a fruitful, abundant life.

Hope is one of my favorite things. It's a mighty force. It can change your attitude and your opportunity. Hope can make you run faster, jump higher, be more creative, endure, push, fight, and win more than almost anything else. We can choose hope, but to do so requires doing battle with the things that steal our hope.

Not seeing can steal hope. But if you've seen something successfully done before, it expands your vision and helps you see farther because you have something to base your perspective on and increase your hope. A plan successfully done by millions of people can help you see farther than your own single experience. That's what the Baby Steps are—a plan that has helped millions successfully build wealth. And not just build wealth for wealth's sake. It's a plan to build wealth *so that* you're able to give outrageously. It's a plan to build wealth *so that* you can have hope and peace for your future and the future of others. I've seen it work for over thirty years. You've seen it within the stats and stories of this book. Maybe you've even seen it work in your own life. If so, that's awesome! Keep going! If not, now is the time to apply the Baby Steps to your own life.

You can do this! You can be a Baby Steps Millionaire! You can retire with dignity and change your family tree. Remember, you're only limited by the size of your hope. And as you grow your hope and your wealth, you can also grow your generosity and your impact. You can pass the hope and the plan on to others. And just think what could happen then!

A Millionaire Movement

Imagine a world full of Baby Steps Millionaires. What would it be like to have Baby Steps Millionaires in every neighborhood, on every rural road and main highway, on every city block and in every small-town square? An all-out millionaire movement! Just think about that!

Imagine the freedom it would bring to your stressed-out neighbors and community leaders. The joy and generous spirit that would spread through the neighborhood and marketplace because no one's constantly trying to "get mine." Everyone would have what they need, and there would be overflow for others. Think about how it would eliminate poverty or a need for the government to "rescue" us. People would be healthier because they could afford the medical care they need. The predatory payday loan industry would shrivel up and die. The puppeteering credit card towers would topple. Student loans would be eradicated with all-cash payments. People wouldn't live paycheck to paycheck and could plan for the future they want, not for the future that their debt dictates to them.

If this were a political book, I would say this is how you beat socialism, and Marxism, consumerism, and all the -isms. But politics has nothing to do with it. It doesn't matter your political affiliation or any other unique detail of your demographic. There's no unique starting point that changes the success of the Baby Steps. The Baby Steps are proven. And hope is contagious. Put them together and a millionaire movement is entirely possible. But it starts with you! This is your pivot point.

You Can Be a Baby Steps Millionaire

To come to the end of this book and not be ready to move the needle on your millionaire goals would be a huge miss. Reading *Baby Steps Millionaire* can give you vision and motivation, but just reading it, snapping a picture of it, and sharing on social media that you've read it, and then putting it back on the shelf isn't going to get you to the millionaire finish line. I've given you the vision for what it could look like in your life and the plan to get there. Now it's time to make the vision your own.

Choose hope over fear and anger. Choose to move forward and take control of your circumstances and your money. Choose to steward your life and your finances in such a way that people can't help but catch hope from you. I want to see you win. With the Baby Steps, I know you can! And I'm not the only one. Jeremiah 29:11 says, "'For I know the plans I have for you,' declares the Lord, 'plans to prosper you and not to harm you, plans to give you hope and a future'" (NIV). God wants and has planned good things for you!

He did not create you to be defeated, discouraged, frustrated, or wandering aimlessly without a plan. His plan is to prosper you. His plan is to give you hope and a future.

So, grab hold of His promises for your life. Reread the stories and the undeniable stats from *The National Survey of Millionaires*. Take a drive like Melanie and JD and listen to millionaire after millionaire share their amazing journeys on *The Ramsey Show*. Dream of how becoming a Baby Steps Millionaire would change the trajectory of your future. Take a *Financial Peace University* class for more accountability, or dog-ear Chapters 2 and 3—the how-to is there. Then lace up your marathon shoes and settle into a steady pace for Baby Steps 4–7.

Be the tortoise and run the long course with intentionality. Be generous along the way. And encourage someone else to Baby Step to a million with you. My team and I will be on the race route cheering for you every mile. And together, we'll build more than wealth. We'll build hope-filled neighborhoods all across this nation full of millionaires who are changing their families and communities, and whose lives scream . . . ***YOU CAN DO THIS TOO***!

———

Better Than I Deserve

So, you've just completed a book about becoming a millionaire. Becoming a millionaire is a great, life-changing goal for you and your family, and obviously, I'm all about showing you how. But I'm definitely not teaching that money is everything or even the main thing.

Money is only valuable because of what it does. When you're in need, it can buy shoes for your children. When you're generous, it can feed other children all over the world. Money can give you control over parts of your life and make your day-to-day more peaceful. For example, new tires on a car are better than a flat on the side of the road. I've had both, and that's how I know money is valuable. Money, however, will not make you happy. Money will not bring you peace. Money will not cause real love or friendship. Money will not secure your eternity. So, while being a Baby Steps Millionaire is a great and worthy goal, it is NOT the main thing.

On my radio show, when people ask me how I'm doing, I always answer: *Better than I deserve*. I don't say that because of money or wealth or what I have. I say that because of the grace of Christ. It's important and worthwhile to build wealth, but one second after you're dead, none of it will matter. I have never seen a Ryder truck following a hearse. The truth is, he with the most toys when he dies is dead. But the grace of Christ can change the ending to the story.

As you've read throughout these pages, my story is not that different from a lot of people in America. I was raised in a middle-class household. I was taught the value of hard work. I graduated from high school, went off to college, got my real estate license at eighteen years old, and decided that was going to be my work-through-college job. I worked forty to sixty hours a week, and I graduated from college in four years.

I've always been that nerdy kid who set goals and measured my success by my ability to accomplish those goals. And so, while I was in college, I thought, *I want to graduate from college in four years*, and I set that as a goal. I thought, *Someday, I want to be a millionaire*, and I set that as a goal. And like a lot of people as they finish college and start their grown-up lives, I thought, *I want to get married and have a family*, so I set that as a goal. And that's exactly what I did. I got married to Sharon two weeks after I graduated from college. The week after our honeymoon, we moved to Nashville and started our new jobs. Everything was a milestone to hit. And we were rolling, just setting and hitting goals, setting and hitting goals. We were full of expectation and full of dreams. We were invincible.

Like I shared in Chapter 5, I started buying and selling real estate, and I got rich, at least by a-kid-from-Antioch-Tennessee standards. I started with nothing, and by the time I was twenty-six, I had $4 million worth of real estate, and a little over a million-dollar net worth. This was back in the '80s, and I was making $250,000 a year, $20,000 a month. I don't know what neighborhood you grew up in, but in the neighborhood I grew up in, we called that *rich*. And it was fun, too! It was another one of those milestones that we were hitting. We were able to buy things and do things like travel. And our marriage was good. Everything was the way it was *supposed* to be.

But of course, you and I both know that life happens, and pain and time tend to steal some of the joy and naiveté—the idea that everything's going to be okay, that everything's going to be perfect. And in the middle of that success, I started getting this sensation that—even though I was acquiring things that I wanted, even though I was winning in business, even though our personal life was good—it wasn't enough. There was a hole. Something was missing. And honestly, it became increasingly troublesome. There was a stirring and indigestion in my spirit. I couldn't figure it out because everything was going the way it was *supposed* to go.

Blaise Pascal said, "There is a God-shaped vacuum in the heart of every man, which cannot be filled by any created thing." And I was trying to satisfy it with created things, with goals, with hitting all the milestones. Most people understand that stuff does not make you happy. And yet, we run around acquiring stuff, acquiring degrees, acquiring milestone after milestone, doing things that are *supposed* to make us happy. Sometimes people try to fill the spiritual vacuum with negative things. They get addicted to drugs, alcohol, pornography, or all kinds of other things. But whether it's just stuff, milestones, drugs, or alcohol, there's only one thing that fits in that God-shaped vacuum perfectly—God.

As I said, I grew up in Antioch, just outside of Nashville. In Nashville, there are more Baptists than people. Practically everybody's a Christian (or pretends to be). I had gone to church a couple of times as a kid, either with some girl I was dating in high school or with my grandmother who drug me by my ear. Every time I went, it didn't seem like people there were having much fun. It didn't seem like church people were people I wanted to be like. But I did know something was missing inside of me.

So as a young professional, I was intrigued when I attended a seminar and the guy teaching got to the end of his talk and said, *You can reach all these milestones and continue to win, but it won't matter if you don't know this man named Jesus. If you don't know Him, you'll never have peace.*

That hit me hard. I didn't know peace, no matter what I seemed to strive to achieve. No matter the goals I hit, it still wasn't enough.

So, I went home and told Sharon that we needed to check out some churches. And she said, "Who are you, and what have you done with my husband?" Like I said, I was not a church guy. Where I come from, Sunday means you drink beer and watch football. I understand that might be offensive to some, but that's how I grew up. Going to church on Sunday? You've got to be kidding! But I was so hungry for the peace the seminar speaker had talked about. So, that was that. We were going to church.

We visited some churches, and we did find some places that were boring. We found some people who were hypocritical, who really didn't seem to care about others but were just going through the motions. We found that there are all kinds of different worship styles and brands of churches. But I really wasn't looking for a church. I was looking for God. And I'm a wide-open, go-all-in kind of guy. So, the real calm church thing? I'm just not that guy. I had to find someplace that fit my wide-open style.

We finally stumbled in the back door of this little church where I saw a lady in the choir loft raising her hand like she knew the answer to some question. Back then, I thought nobody raised their hands in church except in the "crazy churches." I told Sharon, "If they get snakes out, I'm out of here. There's no way I'm sticking around." But I realized the people were actually having fun. And the pastor was a firm, but kind and gentle man. He knew what he believed, and he was comfortable in his own skin.

I began to study and ask questions. And I also had a guy ask me a question. He asked, "What would you say if God asked you, 'Hey, Dave, why should I let you into heaven?'" I, of course, gave the standard answer: "Well, I'm a good guy. I give money to good causes. I'm nice to people most of the time. And I pet puppies. I'm a good guy."

Of course, that's not the answer. And as I continued to study and learn, I found out that God is actually crazy about me. And He's crazy about you. In his writings and teachings, Christian author and speaker Brennan Manning describes how God loves us so much that He calls us *His beloved*. It's an old phrase, but wow, it's powerful. *I am His beloved. He's crazy about me.* That felt different. That was a revelation.

Remember that Jeremiah 29:11 says, "'For I know the plans I have for you,' declares the Lord, 'plans to prosper you, and not to harm you, plans to give you hope and a future'" (NIV). God's not only crazy about you and me, He has a plan for us—a plan for our life and a plan for our eternity. But it begs the question: Do you know for sure where you're going to be in eternity?

In John 10:10, Jesus said this: "I have come that they may have life, and that they may have it more abundantly" (NKJV). Now I knew instantly when I read that, that He was not talking about an abundance of stuff, because I already had an abundance of stuff. He was talking about an abundance of spirit and abundance in my soul, an abundance in my connectivity to my Heavenly Father, who's crazy about me.

Jesus also says in John 14:3, "And if I go and prepare a place for you, I will come again and receive you to Myself; that where I am, there you may be also" (NKJV). This is Jesus telling us He's going to heaven and He's going to build a house right next door to Him, just for me and just for you. As a loving dad and Papa Dave, I get it. I'm *really* happy that my kids and grandkids have homes near me. That's what God did. He built a house for us in heaven, and He's waiting on us. He's made me an heir, and He's made you an heir. It's all planned out.

As I started understanding that He's got a plan for me, the indigestion in my soul started relaxing. I started connecting with something called Truth, and that started to light me on fire. And I realized more and more that all my good deeds aren't enough, but that's okay. Romans 3:23 says, "For all have sinned and fall short of the glory of God" (NKJV). In other words, I've messed up. I'm not perfect. You've messed up, and you know that you're not perfect. Some of us are more messed up than others. The point is, we all mess up, and no amount of striving and achieving changes that. Once I put all my merit badges on the shelf, I realized that there was nothing left but just Dave. And God is crazy about me regardless of my imperfection.

Just doing good things to try to get into heaven is like two guys training to jump across the Grand Canyon. One guy doesn't do a lot of training, and he runs and makes it a few feet, and of course, goes straight to the bottom of the Grand Canyon. Splat. The other guy does a bunch of training, but guess what? You and I know he can't jump across the Grand Canyon. No matter how good of shape he's in, he might make it farther than the other guy, but he still isn't going to make it all the way across. Splat, also.

Trying to jump to heaven based on my good deeds gets me the same result. Being good or even being a better person than the other guy still won't cause me to make it to the other side. Being a Republican won't cause me to make it to heaven. Being a Democrat won't cause me to make it to heaven. Conservatives don't make it to heaven. Liberals don't make it to heaven. No one makes it to heaven except, the Bible says, through the Son. This is great news. As a matter of fact, it's the best news you will ever hear in your entire life.

God is the most pure being in the universe. He's so pure and holy that His very nature cannot tolerate even a speck of anything unclean or imperfect in His presence. Now, this left Him with a dilemma. He's crazy about us and has built a house for us to move into, but He can't tolerate our uncleanness in His presence. So how does He solve this?

He had to come up with a perfect sacrifice. He had to pay the price for us to get into heaven. He built a bridge across the Grand Canyon, so to speak. This is the Christmas story. That baby in the manger, Jesus, is God's only son. John 3:16 tells us, "For God so loved the world, that He gave his only begotten son, that whoever believes in Him should not perish, but have everlasting life" (NKJV).

Now, I've got a son. And I can't grasp the idea that as a dad I would give my son for anyone. But God did that. That's how much He loves me. And that's how much He loves you. John 3:16 makes it clear that, when you believe in Him and you die, you're going to live forever. Of course, Jesus grew up from being that baby in the manger. He became a great teacher and lived a sinless life. And then, according to God's plan, Jesus was crucified, killed on a cross, died, and was buried. And three days later, He got up from the grave on His own power.

It was the perfect sacrifice. Jesus died to pay the price for our misdeeds, our sins, because we don't have the ability to do that on our own. And He had to pay for it with a perfect life. He did it for me, and He did it for you. That's how much He loves you. Whether you choose to walk across this bridge and believe in it is up to you. He doesn't make you accept Him, but He loves you anyway.

When I was twenty-four years old, I decided to cross that bridge. And the process is amazingly simple. All I had to do is realize that I'm not perfect and I'm what the Bible calls a *sinner*. And then I had to say that I'm going to turn away from any known sin and misbehavior. The Bible calls that *repentance*. Repentance means to turn away from misbehavior—not to be perfect, but to turn toward Jesus, place my faith in Him, and believe the story of His great news: He paid this perfect sacrifice for me.

Now, concepts like *repentance* and *sacrifice* and *faith* might be a lot to comprehend, but let's take it in simpler terms. Imagine a chair. We can intellectually discuss, think about, and talk about that chair and whether it will hold us if we sit on it, but it's all theory. It's all just kind of out there and ethereal . . . until you actually sit on the chair. When you sit down on the chair, that's when you've placed your faith in the chair. It's no longer just an intellectual discussion. You make the decision to sit, and the chair holds you.

Faith in Jesus is the same. Faith in Jesus means you accept and believe who He is, that He died and rose for you, that He has a plan and purpose for you. It means you repent from your sin, turn from misbehavior, and turn toward God and His Son, Jesus Christ. When I did that, peace flooded my soul, and I've never had a hole in my soul since. I began to relax, and I found a thing that the Bible calls the *peace that passes understanding* (Philippians 4:7).

Is there any reason anyone wouldn't want that? If you've got that kind of empty place, that indigestion in your spirit, and things just aren't right, then you need the peace of Christ. You need to decide how you would answer this question: Why would God let you into heaven?

Again, the process I went through was:

1. I repented from my sin.
2. I turned away from my misbehavior.
3. I placed my faith in Jesus and decided I'm going to set my life and my eternity on Him.
4. I gave Him control of my life and aligned my values with His.

Romans 10:13 says, "Whoever calls on the name of the Lord shall be saved" (NKJV). I grew up hearing people around Nashville saying so-and-so just got saved. I didn't know what that meant. I thought, *What happened? Saved from what? Was he drowning?* Well, this is what they're talking about. When you give your life to Christ, you get saved from going to hell, saved from living your life with something missing. Your God-shaped hole gets filled by God and God alone.

Maybe you've already been saved. Maybe you accepted Jesus as Lord of your life years ago. Or maybe you kind of moved your life away from it, and something led you to this book about building wealth. If that's the case, maybe it's time for you to recommit your life to Jesus. You can do this again. Whether it's for the first time or the fiftieth time, you can pray this simple prayer and begin to experience the things I'm talking about:

Jesus, I realize that I've sinned against God. I realize that I cannot save myself. I realize that if I got what I deserved, I would live hell on earth and in hell forever. Jesus, I believe that you are the resurrected and living Son of God, who died on the cross for my sins. Jesus, right now, I turn away from my sin, and I ask you to come into my life and take control. Give me eternal and abundant life with you. Jesus, thank you for saving me. Amen.

That's all there is to it. Now, you may or may not experience fireworks in your life because you prayed that prayer. There were no fireworks at my house. I was simply filled with an undeniable peace. But one thing's for sure, the angels are having a big party in heaven right now! The Bible says that there's a heavenly celebration going on every single time someone decides they're going to walk across that bridge and accept Christ as their Savior.

Fireworks or not, you've made a commitment, so there are a couple of things for you to do to continue your learning. I want you to get a good Bible. There's a whole bunch of different translations to choose from. Get one that works for you and begin to study. Begin to learn what God's love letter says to us. It'll change your life. Also, find a good church. You're not going to find a perfect one—there are people in them! But find one where the worship style and preaching style fits your style. Find one where you can ask questions and learn. Find one where you don't feel like the people are looking down on you. And ask them to teach you about baptism. And then, as you learn and grow, ask them to baptize you.

If you said this prayer and you've changed the trajectory of your life, I'd like to hear from you. I want you to go to our website, ramseysolutions.com, and get in contact with us. I promise I won't read your story over the radio, but I'd love to hear from you personally, whether it's an email, snail mail, or social post—whatever it is, just send me a note. I want to know that you did this.

Building wealth is important. But building an eternal relationship with Jesus is everything. It's why I do a lot of the things I do—to have the opportunity to share about the grace and peace of Christ. It's really why I'm *better than I deserve.*

I pray you found this peace that passes understanding and abundant, eternal life in Him. God bless you.

NOTES

1. "Usain Bolt Biography," The Biography.com website, A&E Television Networks, updated May 14, 2021, https://www.biography.com/athlete/usain-bolt.

2. Andrew Keh, "Eliud Kipchoge Breaks Two-Hour Marathon Barrier," *The New York Times*, October 12, 2019, https://www.nytimes.com/2019/10/12/sports/eliud-kipchoge -marathon-record.html.

Aylin Woodward, "Kenyan runner Eliud Kipchoge finished a marathon in under 2 hours, sprinting at a 4:34-mile pace. Here's why his record doesn't count," *Insider*, October 15, 2019, https://www.businessinsider.com/kenyan-marathoner-broke-2-hour-record -doesnt-count-2019-10.

3. "Historical Returns on Stocks, Bonds and Bills: 1928–2020," NYU | Stern, January 2021, http://pages.stern.nyu.edu/~adamodar/New_Home_Page/datafile/histretSP.html.

4. "The 80% Pension Funding Standard Myth," American Academy of Actuaries *Issue Brief*, July 2012, https://www.actuary.org/sites/default/files/files/80_Percent_Funding_IB _071912.pdf

5. Khalid Kal Ghayur and Dwight D. Churchill, *Career Success, Navigating the New Work Environment, Third Edition*, Interview with John C. Bogle, CFA Institute, 2017, pp. 154–159, https://www.cfainstitute.org/-/media/documents/book/career/car-v2017-n3-1.ashx.

6. United States Census Bureau, "Income in the Past 12 Months (in 2019 Inflation-Adjusted Dollars)", https://data.census.gov/cedsci/table?q=United%20States%20Income %20and%20Poverty&tid=ACSST1Y2019.S1901.

7. Katie Warren, "Jeff Bezos is the first person ever to be worth $200 billion. This is how the Amazon CEO's immense wealth stacks up to the average US worker, the

British monarchy, and entire countries' GDP," *Insider*, October 21, 2020, https://www .businessinsidercom/how-rich-is-jeff-bezos-mind-blowing-facts-net-worth-2019-4.

8. Katie Warren, see previous note.

9. Andy Kiersz, Taylor Nicole Rogers, and Hillary Hoffower, "Jeff Bezos plans to step down as Amazon CEO later this year. Here's how he makes and spends his $196 billion fortune," *Insider*, February 2, 2021, https://www.businessinsider.com/jeff-bezos-net-worth -life-spending-2018-8.

10. Andy Kiersz et al, see previous note.

11. Marcia Dunn, "Jeff Bezos blasts into space on own rocket: 'Best day ever!'" *AP News*, July 20, 2021, https://apnews.com/article/jeff-bezos-space-e0afeaa813ff0bdf23c37fe1 6fd34265.

12. Caroline Delbert, "Jeff Bezos Is Building a 10,000-Year Clock Inside a Mountain," *Popular Mechanics*, April 27, 2020, https://www.popularmechanics.com/science/a31156395 /jeff-bezos-clock-long-now-mountain/.

13. Kerry A. Dolan with Chase Peterson-Withorn and Jennifer Wang, "The Forbes 400: The Definitive Ranking Of The Wealthiest Americans In 2020," *Forbes*, August 2020, https://www.forbes.com/forbes-400/.

14. "Mark Cuban Biography," The Biography.com website, A&E Television Networks, updated April 16, 2021, https://www.biography.com/business-figure/mark-cuban.

15. Sam Quinn, "LeBron James will surpass $1 billion in career earnings in 2021, per report," *CBS Sports Digital*, February 11, 2021, https://www.cbssports.com/nba/news/lebron -james-will-surpass-1-billion-in-career-earnings-in-2021-per-report/.

16. Kurt Badenhausen and Mike Ozanian, "NBA Team Values 2021: Knicks Keep Top Spot At $5 Billion, While Warriors Seize No. 2 From Lakers," *Forbes*, February 10, 2021, https:// www.forbes.com/sites/kurtbadenhausen/2021/02/10/nba-team-values-2021-knicks-keep -top-spot-at-5-billion-warriors-bump-lakers-for-second-place/?sh=1dd6a336645b.

17. John Branch, "You Want to Climb Mount Everest? Here's What It Takes," *The New York Times*, December 18, 2017, https://www.nytimes.com/2017/12/18/sports/climb-mount -everest.html.

18. "Clingmans Dome," Great Smoky Mountains National Park, National Park Service website, updated March 4, 2020, https://www.nps.gov/grsm/planyourvisit/clingmans dome.htm.

19. Kerry A. Dolan, Jennifer Wang, and Chase Peterson-Withorn, editors, "Forbes World's Billionaires List: The Richest in 2021," *Forbes*, March 5, 2021, https://www.forbes .com/billionaires/#391dcbae251c.

20. "Coronavirus Reduces Millionaire Count," Spectrem Group, March 23, 2020, https://spectrem.com/Content/millionaire-count-reduces.aspx.

21. Dustin McKissen, "This Study Immigrants are Far More Likely to Start New Businesses Than Native-Born Americans," *Inc.*, February 21, 2017, https://www.inc.com /dustin-mckissen/study-shows-immigrants-are-more-than-twice-as-likely-to-become -entrepreneurs.html.

22. Dane Stangler and Jason Wiens, "The Economic Case for Welcoming Immigrant Entrepreneurs," The Kauffman Foundation, updated September 8, 2015, https:// www.kauffman.org/resources/entrepreneurship-policy-digest/the-economic-case-for -welcoming-immigrant-entrepreneurs/.

23. "Condoleezza Rice," Introduction to Rice's speech to the National Council of Negro Women on December 8, 2001, *American RadioWorks*, American Public Media, http:// americanradioworks.publicradio.org/features/blackspeech/crice.html.

24. Condoleezza Rice, interview by Renee Montagne, *Morning Edition*, NPR, October 13, 2010, https://www.npr.org/templates/story/story.php?storyId=130425923.

25. Condoleezza Rice, interview by Ken Coleman, *EntreLeadership* podcast, Ramsey Solutions.

26. Arlisha R. Norwood, "Condoleezza Rice," National Women's History Museum, 2017, https://www.womenshistory.org/education-resources/biographies/condoleezza-rice.

27. Condoleezza Rice, interview by Ken Coleman, *EntreLeadership* podcast, Ramsey Solutions.

28. Nicholas A. Christakis, M.D., Ph.D., M.P.H., and James H. Fowler, Ph.D., "The Spread of Obesity in a Large Social Network over 32 Years," *The New England Journal of Medicine* 357, no. 4 (2007): 370–379, https://www.nejm.org/doi/full/10.1056/NEJMsa066082.

29. Christakis and Fowler, see previous note.

30. Aaron Shields, "The Odds of Making It To The NFL," Casino.org (blog), May 4, 2021, https://www.casino.org/blog/the-odds-of-making-it-to-the-nfl/.

31. Conner Christopherson, "Patrick Mahomes' Contract Structure is a Blessing for the Chiefs, Curse for the Rest of the NFL," *FanNation*, part of the Sports Illustrated Media Group, March 14, 2021, https://www.si.com/nfl/chiefs/gm-report/kansas-city-chiefs -patrick-mahomes-contract-restructuring-breakdown.

32. Ben Rolfe, "How does the NFL salary cap work in 2021?" *Pro Football Network*, June 2, 2021, https://www.profootballnetwork.com/how-does-nfl-salary-cap-work-2021/.

33. Kurt Badenhausen, "NBA Highest-Paid Players: LeBron James' Career Earnings Will Hit $1 Billion In 2021," *Forbes*, January 29, 2021, https://www.forbes.com /sites/kurtbadenhausen/2021/01/29/the-nbas-highest-paid-players-2021-lebron-curry -durant-score-combined-235-million/?sh=2e2a66026ea2.

34. Pablo S. Torre, "How (and Why) Athletes Go Broke," *Sports Illustrated* Vault, March 23, 2009, https://vault.si.com/vault/2009/03/23/how-and-why-athletes-go-broke.

35. Daniel Roberts, "16% of retired NFL players go bankrupt, a report says," *Fortune*, April 15, 2015, https://fortune.com/2015/04/15/nfl-players-bankrupt/.

36. Andre Rison, *30 for 30*, S:2, Episode 1, "Broke," directed by Billy Corben, ESPN Films, released October 2, 2012.

37. "Andre Rison Net Worth," Celebrity Net Worth website, https://www .celebritynetworth.com/richest-athletes/nfl/andre-rison-net-wort/.

38. Steve McVicker, "Billie Bob's (Mis) Fortune," *HoustonPress*, February 10, 2000, https://www.houstonpress.com/news/billie-bobs-mis-fortune-6565369.

39. Minda Zetlin, "In 2 Words Skiathlete Simen Krueger Explains How He (Literally) Fell on his Face but Won Gold Anyway," *Inc.*, February 12, 2018, https://www.inc.com /minda-zetlin/in-2-words-skiathlete-simen-krueger-explains-how-he-literally-fell-on-his -face-but-won-gold-anyway.html.

40. Associated Press, "Norwegian skier Simen Hegstad Krueger crashes early, breaks pole, still winds gold medal," *USA Today*, updated February 12, 2018, https://www.usatoday

.com/story/sports/olympics/2018/02/11/norways-krueger-wins-gold-in-skiathlon-after-early-crash/110314870/.

41. "Krueger recovers from fall to lead Norway skiathlon sweep," Olympics.com, February 11, 2018, https://olympics.com/en/news/krueger-recovers-from-fall-to-lead-norway-skiathlon-sweep.

42. Minda Zetlin, "In 2 Words Skiathlete Simen Krueger Explains How He (Literally) Fell on his Face but Won Gold Anyway," *Inc.*, February 12, 2018, https://www.inc.com/minda-zetlin/in-2-words-skiathlete-simen-krueger-explains-how-he-literally-fell-on-his-face-but-won-gold-anyway.html.

43. Jack Kelly, "Furloughed Workers Don't Want To Return To Their Jobs As They're Earning More Money With Unemployment," *Forbes*, April 28, 2020, https://www.forbes.com/sites/jackkelly/2020/04/28/furloughed-workers-dont-want-to-return-to-their-jobs-as-theyre-earning-more-money-with-unemployment/?sh=28f19f7f6b76.

44. "People Want to Stay Unemployed Because They Make More Money?!—Dave Ramsey Rant," *The Ramsey Show*, May 20, 2020, https://youtu.be/KXZnxed3E3o.

45. Ramsey+ Whitespace Research, December 2020.

46. "Wealth Inequality is FAIR—Dave Ramsey Rant," *The Ramsey Show*, March 18, 2014, https://youtu.be/X6i8bolkbZA.

47. Chloe Sorvino, "Guy Fieri's New Deal Makes Him One Of Cable TV's Highest-Paid Hosts," *Forbes*, May 23, 2021, https://www.forbes.com/sites/chloesorvino/2021/05/23/guy-fieris-newly-minted-deal-makes-him-one-of-cable-tvs-highest-paid-hosts/?sh=30966e78510f.

48. Emily Ekins, "What Americans Think about Poverty, Wealth, and Work," Cato Institute, September 24, 2019, https://www.cato.org/publications/survey-reports/what-americans-think-about-poverty-wealth-work#a-closer-look-at-young-americans-attitudes-toward-capitalism-wealth-and-the-rich.

49. United States Census Bureau, "Income in the Past 12 Months (in 2019 Inflation-Adjusted Dollars)", https://data.census.gov/cedsci/table?q=United%20States%20Income%20and%20Poverty&tid=ACSST1Y2019.S1901.

50. "How Rich Am I" Methodology, Giving What We Can website, https://www.givingwhatwecan.org/how-rich-am-i-methodology/.

51. "How Rich Am I," see previous note.

52. Hamilton Nolan, "The Forbes 400: A Demographic Breakdown," *Insider* (reprinted from *Gawker*), September 23, 2010, https://www.businessinsider.com/the-forbes-400-a-demographic-breakdown-2010-9.

53. Raymond Bonner, "The Agony of El Salvador," *The New York Times*, February 22, 1981, Archive, https://www.nytimes.com/1981/02/22/magazine/the-agony-of-el-salvador.html.

54. Hisako Sonethavilay, L.S.W. et al., *2018 Blue Star Families Military Family Lifestyle Survey Comprehensive Report* (Syracuse University Institute for Veterans and Military Families, 2018), 10, https://bluestarfam.org/wp-content/uploads/2019/03/2018MFLS-Comprehensive Report-DIGITAL-FINAL.pdf.

———————

The National Study of Millionaires

Contents

Introduction

I'm a math nerd. I love numbers, especially numbers with lots of zeros. I'm also a story-teller. I'm a sucker for a good story. I love hearing people tell their stories, and if you haven't noticed, I love telling a few of my own. I love a story's rise and fall of emotion, its conflict and resolution, and the way it connects people.

C. S. Lewis said, "Friendship is born at that moment when one person says to another: *What! You too? I thought I was the only one!*" When we share our stories, we realize that we have a lot in common. That's what I found over the course of the last thirty years. Sharing my bankruptcy story and the wealth-building turnaround that's come from it has caused people to come forward with their financial stories. And wow, have they come! They've called, emailed, posted, visited, stopped me on the golf course and every place in between to tell me they've paid off debt, built wealth beyond their wildest imaginations, and are changing their family trees. I *love* these stories! It's stories like these that prompted *The National Study of Millionaires* in the first place.

In 2017, we recognized that this flood of wealth-building and millionaire stories began to collide with a larger cultural narrative. The narrative suggested that a slower economy and limited opportunities made it harder for the average person to get ahead financially—much less acquire a $1 million net worth. At the same time, we recognized it had been twenty-five years since Dr. Thomas Stanley conducted his groundbreaking study that set the standard in millionaire research. Stanley's book, *The Millionaire Next Door*, featured the study's findings and made a significant impact on the finance space for over two decades. It served as a road map to financial independence for many. But twenty-five years later, in the middle of an economic decline, a lot of people wondered if Stanley's principles still worked.

So, our research team at Ramsey Solutions set out to find the answers with *The National Study of Millionaires*. We wanted to determine how millionaires gained their wealth and what factors were necessary for the average person in America to reach millionaire status. It became the largest, most statistically significant research project of its kind ever conducted.

All of those anecdotal stories we received at Ramsey through the years led to our working hypothesis for the study: *Millionaires gain wealth on their own through specific choices, such as working hard, demonstrating financial discipline, and investing consistently and wisely over time.* For more than two decades, we had taught these behaviors. So, in addition to identifying what was happening in the wider culture, the study would also help determine if we should continue teaching these behaviors.

On the flip side, we based the study's null hypothesis (a fancy term for a statement that's thought to be true unless it can be shown to be incorrect beyond a reasonable doubt) on the cultural assumptions we had identified: *Millionaires build wealth through advantages not available to most people, including large inheritances, luck, family backgrounds, prestigious educational backgrounds, and large salaries.*

Basically, *The National Study of Millionaires* showed us what happens when the stories and the numbers collide. And there's nothing better than when the numbers tell the story—because the numbers don't lie! When you strip a story down to the numbers, the data shines a light on the rock-solid truth. That's what *The National Study of Millionaires* is about: identifying the truth about millionaires—who a typical millionaire is and what their lifestyles and habits are. And you'll see that the numbers tell a very different story from what the culture would like you to believe. It's an undeniably true story of over ten thousand millionaires—and a shockingly attainable one.

On practically every page of *The National Study of Millionaires*, you'll see your life and habits in the data. Our team has done the due diligence to break the research down based on demographics, family backgrounds, behaviors, characteristics, mindset, and societal

‌‌‍‌‍‍‍‍‍‌‍

‍‍‌

beliefs. Plus, the study gives special insights about millionaire tendencies when it comes to cars, debt, savings, spending, investing, and inheritances.

Read on and let the numbers tell *your* story. Not only CAN you be a millionaire, but by following the Baby Steps, you WILL be a millionaire—and faster than you think.

Research Methodology

Research Overview

The research for *The National Study of Millionaires* included four phases. In the first phase, more than 50 random millionaires were interviewed to collect qualitative data. This information was used to shape the survey that collected quantitative data for the next phase of the research.

In the second phase, the research team examined the results of the interviews and developed the quantitative survey. This survey tool was distributed to 2,000 randomly sampled millionaires. The data gathered from these individuals represented the primary research for the study and were used to determine the validity of the working hypothesis. It should be noted that these millionaires were drawn from "white space"—individuals not affiliated with Ramsey Solutions—to help ensure that convenience bias was not an issue.

The third phase of the project focused on millionaires who were part of the Ramsey Solutions "tribe." Eight thousand millionaires who were members of various Ramsey Solutions email lists, along with individuals who responded to requests made during *The Ramsey Show* radio programs, were included in this phase.

Since this was a convenience sample drawn from the Ramsey audience, the main purpose of this phase was to compare and contrast their responses with data collected from the white space. While a great deal of similarity existed between the two groups, the 2,000 randomly sampled white space responses were given greater emphasis in the book and in validating the working hypothesis when the data diverged.

The final phase of the study involved a random sample of 2,000 people from the general population. This provided a way to compare the characteristics of millionaires with the habits and lifestyles of those who are not millionaires. Being able to compare millionaires with the general population also allowed the research team to address the question of survivorship bias.

In some cases, the research team was able to collect general population data from larger, recognized sources, such as the U.S. Census Bureau, the Bureau of Labor Statistics, and other government data sources. When this demographic information or general data was available, the team relied on that information. When such information could not be located in a broad, general database, the team used the random sample from the general population study.

Qualitative Interviews

As noted, the initial phase of *The National Study of Millionaires* involved a qualitative study of millionaires. The interviews in this phase allowed the research team to determine key topics and insights that could be used to create a valid quantitative survey instrument for the primary focus of the study.

It should be emphasized that the research team recognized the importance of random sampling and made that a priority from the earliest stages of the project. Toward that end, the team began by vetting a number of outside panel providers who could recruit, profile, and activate studies for both the specific population of millionaires and for the general population. As part of the vetting process, the research team narrowed the list of potential providers down to three and, eventually, to one nationally recognized and respected group.

The panel providers were given initial instructions to identify a sample of at least 50 millionaires from across the country for the qualitative portion of the study. They also were given parameters about how "millionaire" should be defined for the purposes of this research, since the term can mean different things to different people. For example, some define millionaires as those earning $1 million a year while others define them as having "liquid" assets equaling $1 million on hand.

The research team chose to include only net-worth millionaires. This definition includes anyone whose assets minus liabilities equal at least $1 million. Financial independence served as a key driver for the research, and the team believed that "net worth" provides the best indicator for such independence.

The research team identified 53 randomly selected millionaires for the qualitative interviews. These individuals were compensated for their participation, receiving $100 in exchange for their responses. The interviews were conducted by telephone between August 11, 2017, and September 8, 2017. At least two researchers were present for each conversation. One researcher served as a moderator, while a second researcher noted responses. The interviews were also recorded for later content analysis.

Each interview lasted at least 60 minutes and provided both autobiographical and sociological data points. The millionaires were encouraged to share details of their early lives, as well as information on their career history. This gave researchers an opportunity to understand the millionaires' personal backgrounds and the role employment played in reaching millionaire status. Researchers also asked the participants about their financial habits and what they believed to be the key factors in becoming a millionaire. This part of the interview focused on things that helped them reach their goals, along with obstacles they had to overcome.

Researchers also encouraged the millionaires to share their thoughts on topics such as philanthropy and retirement, habits and routines, and hobbies and interests. After each interview was completed, its audio file and digital notes were saved. A researcher wrote a brief synopsis of the interview, and key terms were tagged as part of the process. Once all the interviews had been completed, common themes were identified and used to guide the next phase of the project: survey development for the quantitative stages.

Quantitative Design and Sampling

Maintaining the integrity of *The National Study of Millionaires* was a primary concern for the research team throughout the process. For example, the use of qualitative interviews to guide survey development for later quantitative research represents a best practice in statistically significant research. Such interviews allow researchers to identify common themes and pain points within the target audience, which strengthens the viability of the quantitative research instrument.

Content analysis of the qualitative interviews provided direction for the development of the survey questions. The research team spent two weeks in September 2017 writing possible questions and grouping them based on topic and general flow. Throughout the rest of the month, the survey questions underwent a series of stages and gates through which the team refined them and moved them toward final approval. The early days of October 2017 were dedicated to questionnaire testing and refinement. A selection of millionaires from the Ramsey Solutions audience was used to validate the questionnaire and provide additional feedback.

Once the questionnaire was finalized, the panel providers identified 1,000 randomly selected millionaires from outside the Ramsey Solutions audience for distribution. This list included individuals from across the nation and fit the definition of net-worth millionaires. While it was agreed that this sample would provide statistical significance and maintain the study's integrity by keeping the results within a +/- 3% margin of error, Ramsey Solutions also desired the largest research population possible. With that in mind, an additional 1,000 millionaires were added to the random sample.

To further strengthen the sampling process, the panel providers used an invitation-only, double opt-in process. Once potential study participants were identified and vetted, they were extended an invitation to join the project. To join, the millionaires had to accept the invitation and complete a second opt-in feature to provide additional vetting and validation of their qualifications to participate in the study.

Questionnaire Categories

The questionnaire used for the quantitative stages of *The National Study of Millionaires* included 119 questions. Of those, 115 were distributed across eight general categories.

Four additional screener questions were added to strengthen the vetting process. The general categories were broken down as follows:

- Childhood Background (14 questions)
- Family/Relationships (9 questions)
- Career History (10 questions)
- Purchasing/Money Habits (22 questions)
- Achieving High Net Worth (12 questions)
- Myths about Millionaires (10 questions)
- Millionaire Characteristics (30 questions)
- Demographics (8 questions)

The eight general categories were developed through analysis of the qualitative interviews and were designed to help the research team better understand the factors that have influenced—and continue to influence—the financial lives of millionaires. Below is a brief summary of what each category sought to define.

1. **Childhood Background**: The questions in this category sought to delve into the socioeconomics of the participants' upbringings. This included their parents' work histories and their families' standards of living growing up (i.e., upper class, middle class, lower class, and so forth). Researchers also sought to understand the family dynamics of the millionaires' backgrounds, such as whether they came from a divorced or intact family unit and how many siblings they had. They were also asked to describe their educational experiences, including their college choices and their college grade point averages (GPAs), if they had attended college.

2. **Family/Relationships**: The questions in this category examined the millionaires' current family structures. In addition to their ages, the participants were asked to give special focus to their marital status. For members of the sample who were married (a large percentage of participants), researchers encouraged them to share how long they have been married and to rate their marriage (i.e., great, good, okay,

in crisis). Millionaires were also asked how many children they had and, when appropriate, their children's ages.

3. **Career History**: The questions in this category focused on what millionaires do for a living. The survey asked them to share their primary occupation and how long they had been in that profession. Questions about salary history included three sub-categories: by decade (1970s–2010s), by individual earning, and by household earning. Millionaires were also asked to describe their level of passion toward their work.

4. **Purchasing/Money Habits**: The questions in this category considered the way the millionaires in the study have handled their resources in the past and how they currently manage their money. Topics included past vehicle and home purchases, as well as budgeting and spending issues. Participants were asked about their primary expenses each month and what kind of debt they have had or continue to carry.

5. **Achieving High Net Worth**: The questions in this category examined the methods participants used to attain millionaire status. In addition to listing the value of their assets and liabilities to determine estimated net worth, the millionaires were asked about their financial planning practices and what they perceived to be the major factors in their ability to reach financial independence. This included topics such as investing strategies, inheritances, savings habits, real estate assets, and utilizing a professional advisor.

6. **Beliefs about Millionaires**: The questions in this category asked participants to discuss some common cultural beliefs about how millionaires build their wealth. The members of the millionaire sample were asked to rate their responses to the following perceived beliefs:

- Millionaires inherit their wealth.
- Millionaires use debt to build wealth.
- Millionaires use large incomes to build wealth.
- Millionaires experience more luck than average people.

Participants were also asked to use a five-point Likert scale ranging from "strongly disagree" to "strongly agree" to describe their response to the following statement: "If you're born into a poor family, you can't become wealthy."

7. **Millionaire Characteristics**: The questions in this category related to the personal qualities of each millionaire in the study. Researchers asked participants to describe such things as their attitudes toward setting goals and personal disciplines. They were also asked about personal values and motivations, as well as their approach to lifelong learning.

8. **Demographics**: The questions in this category covered the typical personal information for this type of category. Topics such as gender, age, and city of residence were included.

Additional Quantitative Research

As noted above, the core of the research was based on questionnaires distributed to a random sample of 2,000 millionaires from across the country. These millionaires were enlisted by a third-party panel provider and had no prior relationship with Ramsey Solutions. They were carefully vetted prior to receiving the survey questionnaire in an effort to provide the research with the greatest degree of statistical significance possible.

In addition, the research team was curious about how the results from the white space participants would compare to the actions and attitudes of millionaires within their own "tribe." To answer this question, the researchers added a third phase to the project using an 8,000-member convenience sample drawn from a group that has become known as "Ramsey Millionaires." These individuals were recruited from various database lists owned by Ramsey Solutions, as well as callouts from *The Ramsey Show* radio program.

Again, it should be noted that the responses from this sample, while larger than the white space sampling, were used only for comparison purposes. In general, the random sample of millionaires and the convenience sample of Ramsey Millionaires showed alignment in many areas. However, where the two groups differed, the research team deferred to the random sample to maintain the study's integrity and statistical significance.

For example, the two groups showed discernable differences in the area of debt history. As one might expect, many millionaires who were part of the Ramsey Solutions audience began with a larger amount of debt and worked their way through Dave Ramsey's 7 Baby Steps to build wealth over time. As a result, their debt history was far different from the white space millionaires who learned to avoid debt early in life and never had to overcome that obstacle in building wealth. In that case, the researchers leaned heavily on the random sample and referred to the Ramsey Millionaires only as a point of comparison.

Finally, the research team completed a fourth phase of the study by enlisting a random sampling of 2,000 non-millionaires. This group served as a general population sample that could be used for additional comparisons. The research team wanted to avoid survivorship bias, which occurs when data collection focuses only on a given target population (net-worth millionaires) and ignores those outside the target (non-millionaires). The random general population sample addressed this concern.

When possible, the research team also made use of generally recognized sources that typically have extensive and respected databases, such as census data and other government reports. When databases that included comparative information could not be found, the team depended on the random sampling of the general population.

Summary of Results

A team of four researchers from the Ramsey Solutions research team worked to analyze the results collected from the quantitative phases of the research. From that analysis, along with coded information drawn from the qualitative interviews, the team developed several assets. Upon conclusion of that asset creation, the other members of the research team worked with the Ramsey Solutions editorial team to develop a statistically significant narrative of millionaires in America. This collaboration took place throughout 2018.

Millionaire Demographic Information

The 2,000 randomly sampled participants in the study represented a variety of age groups. They also were drawn from every region of the country. The information in the following sections reveals some key demographic data about the millionaires in the study, especially in relation to age and geography.

Millionaires' Ages

The average millionaire in this study was 63 years old. As **Figure 1** demonstrates, a vast majority of those who had attained millionaire status were at least 45 years old. Only 7% were younger than 45, while almost three-fourths of the millionaires were at least 55 (74%).

Figure 1 Age Distribution of Millionaire Study Participants

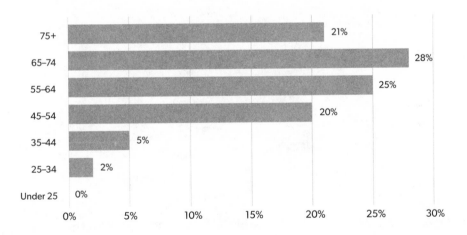

The research team expected this finding. It takes time for individuals to rise to millionaire status, so it should not be surprising that most of these individuals are older. While the sample did include some 20-something or 30-something millionaires, their numbers pale in comparison to those who have spent more time in the workforce earning and investing money.

From a generational perspective, the results were essentially the same. Only 2% of the millionaires in the study were Millennials and 18% were from Generation X. The vast majority of participants were members of the Baby Boomer (54%) and Silent (26%) generations. While social researchers often differ on the precise definitions and ranges of these generational groups, it seems safe to state that more millionaires are members of older generations than younger generations.

But this does not mean that members of younger generations do not have the potential to become millionaires at some point. They may just need more time to earn and invest money so they can build more wealth. This research indicates that if members of younger generations are diligent over time, they can become millionaires in their own right.

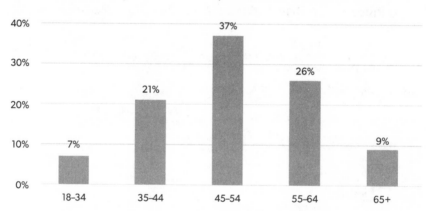

Figure 2 Age When Participants Became Millionaires

As *Figure 2* reveals, more than one-third of the millionaires in the study (37%) said they reached that status between 45–54 years old. Another 26% became millionaires between 55–64 years old. Only 7% were millionaires by the time they were 34.

Interestingly, only 9% of the respondents stated that they became millionaires after the age of 65. Stated another way, more than nine out of 10 millionaires reached financial independence before the traditional age of retirement and the start of Social Security payouts. These findings suggest that individuals should focus on making wise financial decisions during their prime earning years (approximately 35–64), because it is much more difficult—though not impossible—to reach millionaire status after turning 65.

Millionaires' Geography

The participants in *The National Study of Millionaires* were drawn from all 50 states and the District of Columbia. ***Figure 3a*** shows where the 2,000 randomly sampled participants in the quantitative phase live.

Figure 3a Geographic Distribution of Millionaires

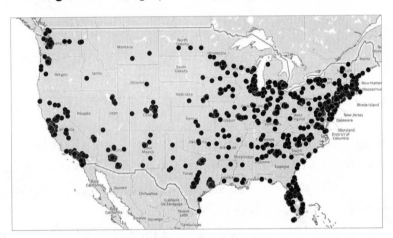

To further examine the millionaires in the study through a geographical lens, the research team used a funnel design to process findings, beginning with broader geographic orientations and drilling down to more personal levels. For example, ***Table 3b*** shows the distribution of participants from a regional perspective. The percentages indicate that distribution was essentially divided evenly across the four major regions recognized by the U.S. Census Bureau: Northeast (22%), Midwest (21%), South (29%), and West (28%). Each region includes the following states:

- **Northeast**: Connecticut, Maine, Massachusetts, New Hampshire, New Jersey, New York, Pennsylvania, Rhode Island, Vermont

- **Midwest**: Illinois, Indiana, Iowa, Kansas, Michigan, Minnesota, Missouri, Nebraska, North Dakota, Ohio, South Dakota, Wisconsin
- **South**: Alabama, Arkansas, Delaware, Florida, Georgia, Kentucky, Louisiana, Maryland, Mississippi, North Carolina, Oklahoma, South Carolina, Tennessee, Texas, Virginia, West Virginia[1]
- **West**: Alaska, Arizona, California, Colorado, Hawaii, Idaho, Montana, Nevada, New Mexico, Oregon, Utah, Washington, Wyoming

Table 3b Geographic Regions of Millionaires

Region	Millionaires	U.S. Census	Difference
Northeast	22%	17%	+5%
Midwest	21%	21%	0%
South	29%	38%	-9%
West	28%	24%	+4%

When compared to the distribution of the general population of the United States, three of the four regions demonstrated relatively similar levels of representation. The comparative distribution in the Midwest was essentially even, while the West (+4%) and the Northeast (+5%) showed slight overrepresentation of the random sample of millionaires. The one significant difference was found in the South, where 38% of the nation's general population lives. However, only 29% of the millionaires who participated in this study live in the South (-9%).

Moving down the funnel from a regional comparison to state distribution, *Table 3c* shows the states in which the concentration of the study's random sample of millionaires is highest when compared to the general population. Or stated another way, these are the states in which more millionaires live than is statistically expected based on the distribution of the nation's general population.

---

[1] The District of Columbia (Washington, D.C.) was included with Virginia and Maryland in the South region.

Table 3c Top 10 Millionaire States by Population Index

Rank	State	% of Millionaires	% of US Population
1	Arizona	3.78%	2.15%
2	Connecticut	1.92%	1.10%
3	Vermont	0.33%	0.19%
4	Hawaii	0.73%	0.44%
5	Massachusetts	3.05%	2.11%
6	Maryland	2.58%	1.86%
7	Illinois	5.37%	3.93%
8	New Jersey	3.71%	2.76%
9	Colorado	2.25%	1.72%
10	Minnesota	2.19%	1.71%

So, for example, approximately 3.78% of all millionaires in the study's random sample live in Arizona. However, only 2.15% of the nation's general population lives in that state. Therefore, the concentration of Arizona millionaires in the random sample exceeds what might be expected given Arizona's percentage of the general population. This is true to varying degrees for every state on this list.

It should be stated again that the millionaire numbers on this table refer only to those who participated in *The National Study of Millionaires*. As such, care must be taken when attempting to extrapolate a given state's universal population of millionaires. However, since the study used a representative random sample, it is reasonable to believe that the study's findings provide generally reliable information about the overall distribution of millionaires in each state.

In contrast to overrepresentation, *Table 3d* shows the other end of the millionaire spectrum. In these states, the concentration of the study's millionaires is much lower than what might be expected from the statistical distribution of the general population. While the overrepresented states were widely distributed, the underrepresented states appear to focus around the interior of the nation.

Table 3d Top 10 States Underrepresented by Millionaires

Rank	State	% of Millionaires	% of US Population
41	Tennessee	0.86%	2.06%
42	Montana	0.13%	0.32%
43	Alabama	0.60%	1.50%
44	Wyoming	0.07%	0.18%
45	West Virginia	0.20%	0.56%
46	Kentucky	0.46%	1.37%
47	South Dakota	0.07%	0.27%
48	Oklahoma	0.27%	1.21%
49	Mississippi	0.13%	0.92%
50	Idaho	0.07%	0.53%

Moving another level down the funnel, the research team examined the distribution of the study's millionaires by zip code. The research produced the following distribution:

- **Urban/Large Metropolitan**: 22%
- **Suburban/Residential**: 63%
- **Rural/Small Town**: 15%

These numbers seem to validate the thesis that a vast majority of millionaires are everyday people who live "normal" lives. Instead of living in fancy townhouses or condominiums in big cities, most of these individuals and their families live in the suburbs—close to, but clearly outside, large urban areas. To use Dr. Thomas Stanley's terminology, they are still "millionaires next door."

These findings are further validated in **Figure 3e**. Drilling down to what could be considered a street level, the research team discovered that the millionaires in this study live in relatively modest homes located in ordinary neighborhoods. The U.S. Census

Bureau states that the average square footage of the new American home is around 2,660 square feet.[2] *The National Study of Millionaires* found that the random sample's average home size is actually slightly smaller at 2,600 square feet.

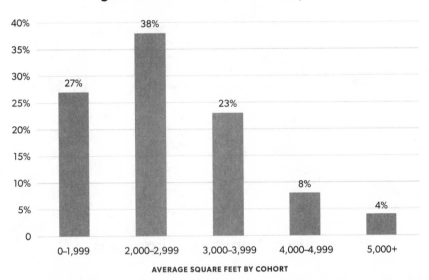

Figure 3e Millionaires and Primary Residence

AVERAGE SQUARE FEET BY COHORT

When the participants' responses are broken down by category, two-thirds of millionaires (65%) live in a home that measures no more than 2,999 square feet. Another 23% have homes that are between 3,000–3,999 square feet. So, the majority of these millionaires and their families are not living in mansions or even larger homes.

In addition to modest homes, the zip code analysis suggests that the millionaires in this study also tend to live in modest neighborhoods. As ***Figure 3f*** demonstrates, more than half of these millionaires (51%) live in neighborhoods where the average family income is less than $75,000. This includes 16% who live in neighborhoods where the average family income is less than $50,000. Only one in five (21%) live in a neighborhood where the average family income exceeds $100,000.

---

[2] United States Census Bureau, "Annual Characteristics of New Housing," 2017.

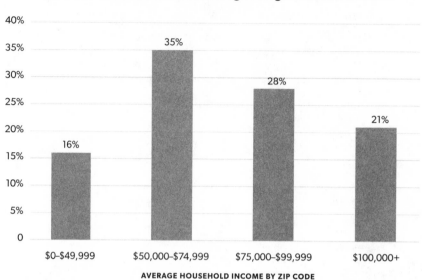

Figure 3f Millionaires and Average Neighborhood Income

AVERAGE HOUSEHOLD INCOME BY ZIP CODE

Millionaires' Family Background

Family of origin has an incredible impact on the life of each individual. Understanding the power of someone's background can provide others with more insight into what that person does or believes. That being the case, the research team wanted to know more about the backstory of the Everyday Millionaires participating in the project. A summary of these findings from their childhood experiences is found below, along with information related to their educational achievements.

Millionaires' Family

As noted elsewhere in the paper, few of the millionaires in the National Study of Millionaires received a substantial inheritance as they built wealth. One possible explanation for this can be found in *Figure 4a*. Among the participants in the study, only 21% came from upper-class or upper-middle-class families as defined by the U.S. Census Bureau. In contrast, approximately three out of every four (75%) were raised in families considered middle class or lower-middle class.

It is worth noting that more participants in the study came from lower-class families (4%) than from upper-class families (2%). In fact, nearly one out of every three participants in the study grew up in "working-class" families (lower class and lower-middle class), yet they managed to reach millionaire status. This finding supports the general belief that anyone can overcome obstacles and become an Everyday Millionaire.

Figure 4a Income Class of Millionaires' Household During Childhood

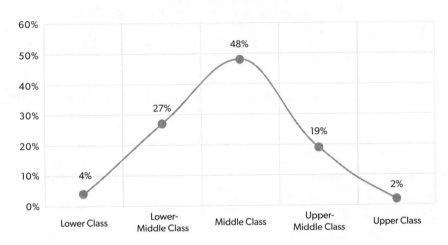

The millionaires in the study also came from homes with a wide variety of parental education and occupations. As **_Figure 4b_** demonstrates, nearly half (47%) of the millionaires who took part in the survey came from homes where neither parent graduated from college or trade school. In contrast, only one in four came from homes where both parents earned a college degree.

Figure 4b Education Level of Millionaires' Parents

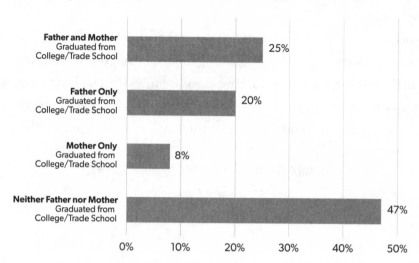

Likewise, the millionaires' parents pursued a variety of professions. The top five occupations of the parents include the following (in no particular order):

- Sales
- Small-Business Owner
- Engineer
- Farmer
- Accountant

The presence of engineers and accountants on this list indicates the rise of white-collar professions over time. The predominance of an agrarian society began its decline several decades ago, and the impact has been seen in the evolution of nonagricultural jobs.

But the transition was not complete during the childhood years of many Everyday Millionaires. Farmers are still present in the list, indicating that agriculture still had a powerful impact on the early lives of many millionaires. In addition, it may be argued that sales and small-business ownership looked much different during the millionaires' childhoods than they do today. For many, someone in sales worked in a smaller local store or sold items door to door. Likewise, small businesses dotted the landscape of small-town America a few decades ago. Instead of the fast-paced technology start-ups, many entrepreneurs in that generation served their communities as tailors, butchers, barbers, grocers, and florists.

Millionaires' Education

When examining their own academic histories, the millionaires in *The National Study of Millionaires* again paint a picture of ordinary lives. As ***Figure 5a*** shows, more than a third of the millionaires in the study were B students, while one in 10 were C students. These results indicate that while the millionaires were generally solid students in high school, their performance was typical of other students.

Figure 5a Millionaires and Type of Student

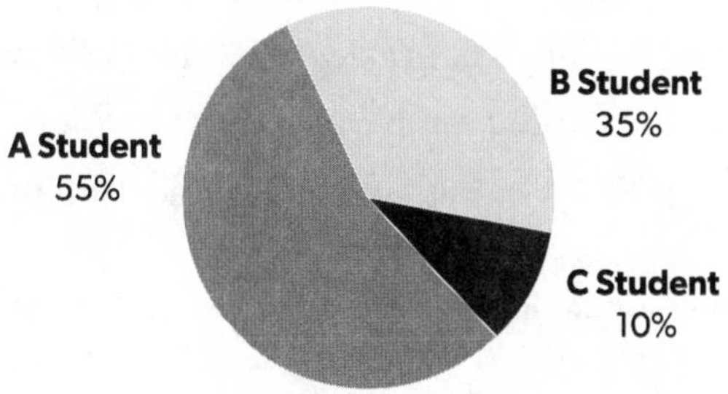

In further support of this "average" lifestyle, ***Figure 5b*** shows that most of the study's millionaires (78%) were involved in extracurricular opportunities during their high school years. Sports and cheerleading provide the largest response in the research at 40%, but other categories are also well-represented. Service clubs (20%), student council (18%), academic teams (17%), band (17%), and the school newspaper (15%) were all reported by at least 15% of participants.

Figure 5b Millionaires and High School
Extracurricular Activities

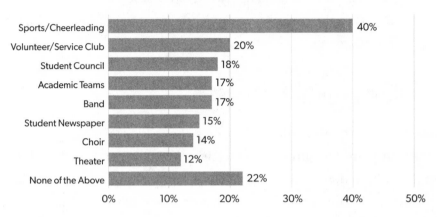

After high school, a vast majority of Everyday Millionaires moved on to receive some level of college education. As **_Figure 5c_** reveals, only 2% of the surveyed millionaires stopped their formal education with a high school diploma or GED, while another 8% took some college classes without getting a degree. A few (3%) graduated with a two-year degree, but most millionaires in the study earned either a four-year bachelor's degree (36%) or graduate degree (38%). More than one in 10 (13%) went on to receive a doctorate.

Figure 5c Millionaires and Level of Education

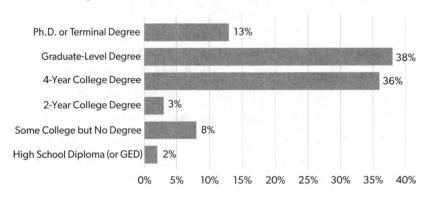

As noted above, many of these millionaires came from homes where neither parent earned a college degree. In fact, 46% of the millionaires in the study were first-generation college graduates. Their academic success also demonstrates a higher level of education than is found in the general population. While 51% of Everyday Millionaires earned a master's degree or doctorate, only 4% of the general population did the same.

These millionaires also studied a variety of majors during their college experiences. While several pursued degrees in the business field, the sciences were also represented, along with education. *Table 5d* shows an alphabetic list of the top 10 degrees earned by participants in *The National Study of Millionaires*:

Table 5d Top 10 Degrees Earned in College

Accounting	Education
Biology	Engineering
Business Administration	Finance
Computer Science	Political Science
Economics	Psychology

The research team found that 62% of participants in the study attended public state universities. In addition, only 7% averaged more than $200,000 a year over the course of their careers. So, the research indicates that high-end educations and high-paying jobs are not the route most participants in the study took to reach millionaire status. Instead, they appear to be primarily normal people with normal backgrounds pursuing normal careers. Rather than experiencing overnight success, they are common folks who worked uncommonly hard over time to reach their goals.

Millionaires' Net Worth

By definition, all the participants in *The National Study of Millionaires* had a seven-figure net worth. As noted, this was calculated by adding the value of all assets and subtracting the value of all liabilities. Assets included things such as homes, vehicles, investments, retirement accounts, and savings accounts. Liabilities included credit card debt, lines of credit, car loans, student loans, and personal loans.

The median net worth for all the millionaires in the study was $2,485,000. **Figure 6a** provides a breakdown of the millionaires in the study based on net worth. Nearly two-thirds (61%) have a net worth of less than $3 million, including 33% with a net worth between $1–2 million. Approximately one in 10 study participants have a net worth exceeding $5 million.

Figure 6a Total Net Worth of Millionaire Study Participants

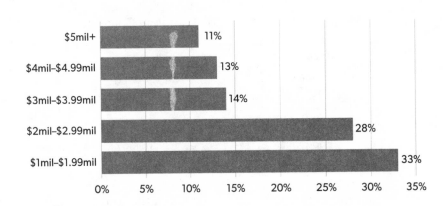

Of course, this does not represent future growth. It is possible that study participants could continue growing their wealth and move into higher net-worth brackets in the years to come.

Along with measuring their net worth, participants were asked about factors that contributed to achieving this wealth. Likewise, members of the randomly sampled general population group were asked about factors they perceived as helping millionaires reach that status.

As **Table 6b** and **Table 6c** show, both groups agreed that financial discipline is the most important factor in building a million-dollar net-worth portfolio and that real estate investments were the least important factor. However, millionaires and the general population diverge greatly from there.

Table 6b

Millionaires and
Building Wealth

Millionaires	Contributing Factor
1	Financial Discipline
2	Investment Consistency
3	Values from Upbringing
4	High-Paying Job
5	Investment Strategy
6	Luck
7	Inheritance
8	Real Estate Investments

Table 6c

General Population and
Building Wealth

General Population	Contributing Factor
1	Financial Discipline
2	Inheritance
3	Investment Strategy
4	Luck
5	High-Paying Job
6	Values from Upbringing
7	Investment Consistency
8	Real Estate Investments

Millionaires in the study stated that investment consistency was the second most important factor in building financial independence, while the general population believes it is only the seventh (out of eight) most important element. Likewise, the millionaires did not place as much value on inheritance (seventh of eight in their list), while the general population felt it was very important (second of eight). Non-millionaires also indicated that luck was relatively important (fourth), while the millionaires ranked it lower on the list (sixth).

In general, the responses indicate that millionaires tend to focus more on elements within an individual's control, while non-millionaires believe financial independence depends on elements outside of an individual's control.

In addition to examining factors necessary to create financial independence, researchers also asked participants about factors that could prevent an individual from reaching millionaire status. **Table 6d** and **Table 6e** provide the breakdown of those responses and reaffirm the differences between how millionaires view building wealth and how the general population views building wealth.

Table 6d
Millionaires and
Preventing Wealth

Millionaires	Contributing Factor
1	Lack of Financial Discipline
2	Consumerism
3	Low-Paying Jobs
4	Debt Levels
5	Lack of Opportunity
6	Cost of Living

Table 6e
General Population and
Preventing Wealth

General Population	Contributing Factor
1	Lack of Financial Discipline
2	Lack of Opportunity
3	Low-Paying Jobs
4	Debt Levels
5	Cost of Living
6	Consumerism

While both groups agreed that a lack of financial discipline makes it most difficult to find financial independence, the study's millionaires rated consumerism as the second greatest concern. In contrast, members of the general population ranked consumerism at the bottom of their list. Non-millionaires were also concerned about a lack of opportunity (second), which millionaires ranked only fifth.

As with the rankings of factors that help create wealth, the responses related to what hinders financial independence reflect a difference of attitude among millionaires in the study and their counterparts in the general population. The study revealed that personal responsibility and diligence were important priorities to the millionaires, so any factor that could derail such internal motivation was seen as a threat to building wealth. Meanwhile, those in the general population indicated that wealth was the product of external forces working on behalf of an individual, so anything that removes those factors from the equation is viewed as an obstacle.

Understanding Behaviors, Characteristics, and Mindset

Identifying Themes from the Research

As noted, the research began with qualitative interviews of more than 50 randomly sampled millionaires from around the country. The information gathered from those interviews was analyzed by the research team to identify common themes and topics that could be explored further in the quantitative phases.

After the interviews and analysis were complete, the research team identified seven major research themes for the quantitative phases. Each of these themes contrasted one action or attitude that helped individuals reach millionaire status with a corresponding action or attitude that did not. It was determined that each of these themes could be integrated into the survey questionnaire and could provide statistically significant data points.

1. **Proactive vs. Reactive.** Based on the research, millionaires tend to be planners and goal-setters. They view things from a long-term perspective, which allows them to weather short-term storms. For example, they understand that saving today is difficult but produces greater benefits in the future. Rather than reacting to people or circumstances in the moment, millionaires stick to proven principles that keep them moving toward the goals they set.

2. **Earned vs. Inherited.** The vast majority of millionaires are self-made individuals. While the stereotype assumes that they were raised in prosperous families, the research indicates that most came from humble beginnings and worked hard over time. Instead of an inheritance, they gained millionaire status through disciplined saving over time and a commitment to lifelong learning. They rely on patience and persistence—not a silver spoon.

3. **Deciding vs. Sliding.** Millionaires in this study demonstrated intentionality with their resources. They chose to "happen" to their money instead of letting their money happen to them. They placed high value on decision-making skills and were convinced that nothing productive—including wealth—ever happens by accident. Even after becoming millionaires, they may appear countercultural.

Their habits create greater financial independence, so they refuse to "slide" along following conventional wisdom.

4. **Coachable vs. Proud/Arrogant**. Millionaires recognize that they do not have all the answers and probably never will. As a result, they are committed to lifelong learning. If they have a question, they are not afraid to seek out the wisdom of someone who has the proper answer. Whether this involves a mentor figure or a professional advisor, millionaires are willing to listen and to use that information to evaluate themselves. Because they are self-aware, millionaires are generally quick to admit their mistakes and to course correct when necessary.

5. **Living Modestly vs. Displaying Wealth**. More than two decades ago, Dr. Thomas Stanley introduced the idea of a "millionaire next door." That is, millionaires are more likely to be a neighbor or coworker than a flashy celebrity. The millionaires in this study demonstrated an aversion to extravagance. Their cars and their homes remain modest. In addition, they continue practicing many of the frugal habits that helped them reach millionaire status: budgeting, using coupons and grocery lists, shopping at discount or second-hand stores, and so forth.

6. **Growth Mindset vs. Fixed Mindset**. Stanford University researcher Dr. Carol Dweck has defined two contrasting mindsets that distinguish people.[3] The first is a fixed mindset through which intelligence is viewed as static. As a result, emphasis is placed on appearing to know something more than actually gaining the knowledge. The second is a growth mindset in which intelligence is constantly developing. As a result, emphasis is placed on continuing to learn and grow. Millionaires tend to demonstrate a growth mindset. Motivated to learn, they accept challenges and overcome obstacles. They develop perseverance. Most importantly, they recognize that embracing an opportunity does not limit the potential of others. To them, opportunities to learn and excel are like candles that can be used to light other candles—not pieces of pie that are gone once consumed.

---

[3] Carol S. Dweck, Ph.D., *Mindset: The New Psychology of Success* (New York: Ballantine Books, 2007).

7. **Owning It vs. Being a Victim**. Based on this research, millionaires take responsibility for their actions and their outcomes. Rather than being carried along by factors outside their control, the participants in this study made it clear that they were the masters of their own destiny. They rejected a victim mentality and were convinced that their success was determined primarily by their own choices and behaviors. As a result, they were convinced that any person could become a millionaire if that person was willing to make the sacrifices now that ensure a secure future.

Creating an Assessment to Verify Qualitative Themes

As the research team analyzed these seven themes, a 30-question assessment was developed to better understand the findings and verify them in the field. The assessment focused on three broad topics that encompass the specific characteristics of wealth building demonstrated by the millionaires in the study. These topics were based on the seven themes identified in the qualitative interviews.

The topics are defined by three specific terms: behavior, knowledge, and mindset. Behavior corresponds to the physical habits that most millionaires weave into their lives to ensure financial independence. These habits may be daily, weekly, or even yearly, but they create regular wins that provide exponential growth over time.

Knowledge corresponds to the millionaires' desire to be lifelong learners. As noted above, the individuals in this study are committed to breaking free from the status quo and to improving over time. They have a desire to learn from mentors and other resources and are not afraid of challenges and obstacles. Most importantly, learning is not an end unto itself; it provides the path for making positive changes in their lives.

Mindset corresponds to the emotional qualities that millionaires see as important to their growth and future stability. These are defined by their core values and principles—the nonnegotiable elements that serve as the foundation for their worldview. Mindset also includes elements such as discipline and the will to take necessary steps toward reaching a goal. This provides the belief and confidence that they could become millionaires and is the basis for their conviction that others can follow the same path toward success.

Understanding these three areas should reveal habits and traits that make millionaires unique. If millionaire status is the result of hard work and discipline—in contrast to inheritances or luck—it's worth noting that time is also a key principle that cannot be ignored. Time and patience stand at the heart of building wealth.

Designing the Assessment

Once the themes were identified, the research team worked to determine how to integrate them into the quantitative research. The key was to imbed a series of relevant statements related to the qualitative themes within the larger body of the survey questionnaire. This allowed researchers to gain useful information about each of the three areas without creating a negative impact on the rest of the study.

Thirty statements were included in the 119 questions of the larger survey instrument. This 30-statement assessment included statements evenly divided between behaviors, knowledge, and mindsets of millionaires. Researchers used a five-point Likert scale format that ranged from "strongly disagree" to "strongly agree." The statements provided weighted averages for each response, with more weight assigned to the higher end of the Likert scale.

In addition to distributing this 30-statement assessment as part of the questionnaire for the random white space sampling of the study, the 2,000 individuals in the general population phase also received the same survey and provided responses. As a result, researchers were able to measure the differences between millionaire perspectives and non-millionaire perspectives on the seven themes and the three areas of study.

The responses, along with comparisons to the general population, will be discussed in the following sections. In these comparisons, anything generally falling within the range of +/-2 was considered "neutral." Anything falling between +3 and +9 was considered "somewhat positive," and anything at +10 or above was considered "positive."

At times, due to specific wording structures, some statements were considered "positive" when the results provided a low or negative correlation. Those exceptions will be noted and explained below.

Behavior Responses

As noted, 10 of the 30 Likert-style statements in the survey instrument related to the behavior and habits of millionaires. *Table 7a* shows the responses to one set of behavior-related statements provided by the 2,000 millionaires in the random white space phase of the study. This set of statements represents five of the 10 statements related to behavior.

Table 7a Weighted Averages for Behavior Statements, Set 1

BEHAVIOR Statements, Set 1	Millionaires	Median	StdDv
I have a long-term plan for my money	4.42	5.00	0.69
I plan for upcoming expenses by saving in advance	4.30	4.00	0.84
I live on less money than I make	4.35	5.00	0.92
I never carry a balance on my credit card	4.70	5.00	0.77
I stick to the budgets I create	3.85	4.00	0.91

As the weighted averages indicate, the responses of the participants to four of the five statements skew very close to "strongly agree." The one exception was a statement about budgets, which still garnered a 3.85, which was closer to "agree." The median score of 4.00 also indicates a strong measure of agreement with the statement in general.

One of the primary findings from this set related to the fourth statement about credit card balances. The weighted average of 4.70 represents the highest average for any statement in the assessment. The result indicates that avoiding consumer debt, specifically balances on credit cards, is one action millionaires believe will lead to financial independence.

As noted, the questionnaire, including the 30-statement assessment, was also distributed to a random sample of 2,000 general population participants. The comparisons between the two groups on this five-statement set are found in **Table 7b**.

Table 7b General Population Comparison
for Behavior Statements, Set 1

BEHAVIOR Statements, Set 1	General Population	Median	StdDv
I have a long-term plan for my money	3.62	4.00	1.13
I plan for upcoming expenses by saving in advance	3.77	4.00	1.07
I live on less money than I make	3.49	4.00	1.18
I never carry a balance on my credit card	3.36	4.00	1.51
I stick to the budgets I create	3.49	4.00	1.02

Across this set, the millionaires' responses demonstrated a positive correlation when compared to the general population. For example, the 4.70 weighted average on the credit card balance statement was 40% higher than the weighted average of the general population. Even the lower 3.85 average on the budgeting statement showed a positive correlation (+10%) when compared to the general population. In scoring higher on five out of five statements, the results indicate that millionaires are more likely to participate in these actions than the average American.

Table 8a shows the responses to the five remaining behavior-related statements. While the weighted averages for these responses are not as large as the first Behavior set, they still fall within "agree." The highest average (4.21 for the fifth statement in the set) indicates that millionaires are highly motivated and demonstrate perseverance over time. They are determined to complete a task once it has been started.

Table 8a Weighted Averages for Behavior Statements, Set 2

BEHAVIOR Statements, Set 2	Millionaires	Median	StdDv
I set aside some of my income every month to give to others	3.47	4.00	1.19
I regularly set personal goals and often write them down	3.11	3.00	1.15
I read approximately one nonfiction book a month	2.88	3.00	1.34
I almost always achieve my goals	3.92	4.00	0.72
If I start something, I finish it	4.21	4.00	0.70

The lowest weighted average for this set involves the habit of reading (2.88), but the median for that statement (3.00) still indicates that an "average" millionaire (half are, half aren't) is reading a book a month and sees it as an important habit for finding success. This correlates with both the "coachable" and "growth mindset" themes, which emphasize lifelong learning.

The information in *Table 8b* generally shows positive correlation for the millionaires, as once again, they score higher than the general population on four out of five statements. The weighted averages demonstrate that while millionaires write down goals, the general population is about as likely to do the same. Millionaires are more likely than the general population to read at least one nonfiction book each month (+12%). The millionaires also are much more intentional about giving and generosity than the general population (+19%).

Table 8b General Population Comparison
for Behavior Statements, Set 2

BEHAVIOR Statements, Set 2	General Population	Median	StdDv
I set aside some of my income every month to give to others	2.92	3.00	1.22
I regularly set personal goals and often write them down	3.11	3.00	1.12
I read approximately one nonfiction book a month	2.57	2.00	1.27
I almost always achieve my goals	3.61	4.00	0.90
If I start something, I finish it	3.90	4.00	0.88

In general, the research reveals that millionaires place a great deal of value on particular habits that they believe will ensure their financial independence. When compared to the general population, these millionaires are more likely to practice these habits than those who have not reached millionaire status.

Mindset Responses

Table 9a shows the responses to one set of statements reflective of a person's mindset. As with the Behavior statements, the millionaires in the random white space sample demonstrated high levels of agreement and strong agreement in these statements.

Table 9a Weighted Averages for Mindset Statements, Set 1

MINDSET Statements, Set 1	Millionaires	Median	StdDv
My friends and family would say I am disciplined	4.29	4.00	0.69
My friends and family would describe me as a hard worker	4.34	4.00	0.70
I do what I think is best, regardless of other people's opinions	4.22	4.00	0.70
At times, I get jealous of my friends/family because of the things they have or get to do	2.14	2.00	1.09
I keep my promises and meet my commitments	4.47	5.00	0.62

With one exception (which will be noted below), the weighted averages for these statements ranged from 4.22 ("I do what I think is best, regardless of other people's opinions") to 4.47 ("I keep my promises and meet my commitments"). As noted, the mindset statements allowed the Ramsey team to dig into the core values and principles that motivate millionaires. These weighted averages indicate that participants hold qualities such as integrity, honesty, hard work, discipline, reliability, and self-determination in high standing.

The one exception from this set relates to feelings of personal jealousy (weighted average of 2.14). This statement represented an "attention filter" for participants. As a best practice, the research team included statements for which the proper response ranked lower ("disagree" or "strongly disagree") on the Likert scale. This ensures that those surveyed are paying attention and not just marking every response high.

In this case, it is expected that millionaires with a proper perspective do not struggle with feelings of jealousy toward friends and family. A "keeping up with the Joneses" mentality can be detrimental to one's personal finance journey. As a result, the expected responses were rated lower ("disagree" and "strongly disagree") on the Likert scale. Both the weighted averages and the median scores provided by the millionaires in this study showed that they were properly engaged with the statements on the survey instrument *and* that jealousy was not an issue with a majority of participants.

The information in ***Table 9b*** again shows a generally positive correlation for millionaires when compared to the general population. The weighted averages indicate that millionaires may view the virtue of discipline as a stronger motivational factor than do non-millionaires (+10%).

Table 9b General Population Comparison
for Mindset Statements, Set 1

MINDSET Statements, Set 1	General Population	Median	StdDv
My friends and family would say I am disciplined	3.91	4.00	0.89
My friends and family would describe me as a hard worker	4.18	4.00	0.83
I do what I think is best, regardless of other people's opinions	4.01	4.00	0.83
At times, I get jealous of my friends/family because of the things they have or get to do	2.67	3.00	1.22
I keep my promises and meet my commitments	4.19	4.00	0.80

The same could also be said to a lesser—but still meaningful—degree of hard work (+4%), self-determination (+5%), and reliability (+7%). So, while both the millionaires and the general population agree that these factors are important, the millionaires are more likely to connect them to personal success—including financial independence—than non-millionaires.

It should be noted that the "attention filter" related to jealousy demonstrated a positive correlation for the millionaires. Since a response on the lower end of the Likert scale represented a healthy perspective, a lower weighted average is considered desirable. With this in mind, the -20% correlation is actually quite positive for the millionaires, indicating that they are much less likely to feel jealousy toward others than members of the general population.

Table 10a shows the responses to the second set of statements related to the area of Mindset. As with the second set of Behavior statements, the weighted averages for these responses are somewhat lower than the first set of Mindset statements. However, they generally do represent a significant level of agreement with the values under consideration.

Table 10a Weighted Averages for Mindset Statements, Set 2

MINDSET Statements, Set 2	Millionaires	Median	StdDv
With hard work and discipline, anyone can become a millionaire	3.59	4.00	1.11
My friends and family would say I am thrifty	3.91	4.00	0.95
I feel pressure to keep up with my friends and family when it comes to money	1.86	2.00	0.92
I am willing to sacrifice to win— even when it's painful	3.16	3.00	1.02
I control my own destiny and am responsible for my future	4.22	4.00	0.76

While its weighted average registered lower than other responses, the virtue of personal sacrifice (3.16) still rated above average among millionaires. The millionaires in the study also affirmed hard work (3.59) and thrift (3.91). The strongest weighted average was related to the statement on self-determination. At 4.22, the millionaires demonstrated a strong reliance on personal responsibility, which indicates a refusal to succumb to a "victim mentality" of any kind. It could be said that they believe in themselves and their own ability to "happen" to life instead of passively allowing things to happen to them.

The statement related to keeping up with the standards of others served as another attention filter for participants. As explained earlier, a response lower on the Likert scale is expected for this statement. So, the weighted average of 1.86 indicates a healthy aversion to what might commonly be called "keeping up with the Joneses." Millionaires tend to define success on their own terms—not by what others around them think or do.

The information in **Table 10b** compares the weighted averages for the millionaire sample to the responses drawn from the general population sample. In these comparisons, millionaires had the strongest positive correlations on the topics of thrift (+10%) and hard work/discipline (+14%). The research responses showed moderate positive correlation for self-determination (+6%).

Table 10b General Population Comparison
for Mindset Statements, Set 2

MINDSET Statements, Set 2	General Population	Median	StdDv
With hard work and discipline, anyone can become a millionaire	3.15	3.00	1.18
My friends and family would say I am thrifty	3.56	4.00	1.06
I feel pressure to keep up with my friends and family when it comes to money	2.43	2.00	1.18
I am willing to sacrifice to win—even when it's painful	3.20	3.00	1.03
I control my own destiny and am responsible for my future	3.99	4.00	0.90

The statement addressing personal sacrifice proved to be one of the few examples of a neutral or negative correlation of millionaires to the general population. The weighted averages of both groups indicate that non-millionaires are slightly more willing to endure sacrifices in the short term if it means success in the long term.

Again, the large difference related to the attention filter ("I feel pressure to keep up with my friends and family when it comes to money") actually represents a positive correlation for the millionaires. The results show that millionaires are 23% less likely to feel pressured to keep up with others. Stated positively, they are much more likely to define their success by their own standards, not the standards of others.

Knowledge Responses

Table 11a shows the responses to the first set of statements correlated to the area of Knowledge. In general, the weighted averages for the Knowledge set were lower than those of the Behavior or Mindset groupings. However, as the median scores reveal, most millionaires "agree" that the qualities and characteristics included in this subset are valuable for building wealth and finding financial independence and show separation between themselves and the general population.

Table 11a Weighted Averages for Knowledge Statements, Set 1

KNOWLEDGE Statements, Set 1	Millionaires	Median	StdDv
I accept and integrate feedback from others	3.91	4.00	0.63
There are some things I am not capable of learning	2.70	4.00	1.07
I will try difficult things to get new results	3.77	4.00	0.72
Challenging myself won't make me any smarter	2.28	2.00	0.92
I am always trying to learn new things	3.93	4.00	0.74

In this first five-statement Knowledge set, the weighted averages tended to hover around "agree" as observed by the median scores. In some instances, though, the research team reverse coded responses, meaning "strongly disagree" and "disagree" were given the greater weight. This method was used for statements stated as negatives to which respondents were expected to respond using the lower end of the Likert scale.

For example, the second statement in the set ("There are some things I am not capable of learning") is stated as a negative, so it is expected that millionaires would provide answers that correlate to the low end of the Likert scale ("strongly disagree" or "disagree"). The weighted average of 2.70 reveals that millionaires are confident (but not arrogant) in regard to their ability to gain new information and learning. This is key to building wealth, as one rarely "has it all figured out."

Likewise, the fourth statement in the set ("Challenging myself won't make me any smarter") is stated in the negative, so a lower response is most healthy and positive. Therefore, the weighted average of 2.28 indicates that the millionaires in the study are essentially confident that they can gain knowledge when appropriately challenged. Many individuals seek to avoid challenges, but millionaires are typically receptive to challenges because they see difficult circumstances as a means of growth and a path to greater success.

In contrast, the first statement ("I accept and integrate feedback from others") and the fifth statement ("I am always trying to learn new things") are worded positively. As a result, the research team expected responses that ranked higher on the Likert scale. Millionaires responded as expected, producing the highest weighted averages in the set at 3.91 and 3.93, respectively.

Table 11b shows a somewhat lower positive correlation between millionaires and the general population. The largest difference between the groups can be found in the weighted average of the second statement ("There are some things I am not capable of learning"). Again, the average of -13% indicates that the millionaires are much more likely to believe they can continue learning throughout life than the general population. This provides a positive correlation when the millionaires are compared to the non-millionaires.

Table 11b General Population Comparison for Knowledge Statements, Set 1

KNOWLEDGE Statements, Set 1	General Population	Median	StdDv
I accept and integrate feedback from others	3.78	4.00	0.76
There are some things I am not capable of learning	3.09	3.00	1.10
I will try difficult things to get new results	3.66	4.00	0.83
Challenging myself won't make me any smarter	2.40	2.00	1.03
I am always trying to learn new things	3.90	4.00	0.83

In the same way, the -5% correlation found in the fourth statement ("Challenging myself won't make me any smarter") is a positive correlation for millionaires. The weighted averages reveal that millionaires are less likely to believe challenges will not help them grow than participants in the general population. Or, stated as a positive, they are more likely to believe that the challenges of life provide valuable learning experiences that can lead them toward financial success.

The responses for the statements related to integrating feedback, trying difficult things, and learning new things could all be considered "somewhat positive" correlations for millionaires compared to non-millionaires.

Table 12a shows the responses to the second set of statements related to Knowledge and the final set of statements in the 30-item assessment. As with the previous Knowledge set, the weighted averages are somewhat lower than in the Behavior and Mindset groupings, but in general, the medians still point toward agreement.

Table 12a Weighted Averages for Knowledge Statements, Set 2

KNOWLEDGE Statements, Set 2	Millionaires	Median	StdDv
I am willing to be wrong and quickly admit to it	3.86	4.00	0.71
My intelligence is something that I can't change very much	2.29	3.00	1.09
If I am not naturally smart in a subject, I will never do well in it	2.41	2.00	0.92
I seek out wisdom from mentors	3.67	4.00	0.86
I am always trying to improve my habits	3.85	4.00	0.75

The first exception is found in the second statement of the set. As mentioned above in discussing the other sets, this statement ("My intelligence is something that I can't change very much") is presented as a negative and was reverse coded by the research team. A response from the lower end of the Likert scale is expected, and the millionaires responded with a weighted average of 2.29. This means that millionaires generally believe their intelligence has the potential to increase over time.

Similarly, the third statement in the set ("If I am not naturally smart in a subject, I will never do well in it") is negative and was reverse coded. The millionaires in the study provided a weighted average of 2.41, meaning they are confident that they can study and master information that was previously unfamiliar to them. Both of these statements are used to show a growth mindset among millionaires, rather than fixed.

The remaining weighted averages in this set are similar, and the median for each of these statements is 4.00. This indicates a high level of agreement on each subject.

Table 12b includes results that will look similar to the comparisons in other sets. The first and fifth statements produced "Somewhat Positive" correlations for millionaires when aligned with the corresponding responses from the general population. However, the fourth statement ("I seek out wisdom from mentors") produced a neutral correlation that slightly favored the general population. In simpler terms, the research found that members of the general population are perhaps more likely to rely on mentors than millionaires. But the difference between the two is not substantial.

Table 12b General Population Comparison for Knowledge Statements, Set 2

KNOWLEDGE Statements, Set 2	General Population	Median	StdDv
I am willing to be wrong and quickly admit to it	3.71	4.00	0.86
My intelligence is something that I can't change very much	2.69	3.00	1.07
If I am not naturally smart in a subject, I will never do well in it	2.50	2.00	1.00
I seek out wisdom from mentors	3.73	4.00	0.89
I am always trying to improve my habits	3.83	4.00	0.78

The second and third statements of the set follow the pattern of previous negatives. Millionaires rated those statements low on the Likert scale, and those responses were much lower than the responses provided by the general population. Therefore, the negative correlations (-17% for the second statement and -4% in the third) are interpreted as positive correlations for the millionaires.

Conclusions from the Assessment

When all 30 statements in the assessment are considered, the weighted averages of the 2,000 randomly sampled net-worth millionaires were consistently higher than the corresponding scores from the random sampling of general population participants. In 27 of the 30 items, the millionaires ranked higher than the general population. Therefore, the research indicates that millionaires are more likely to practice specific behaviors, own particular beliefs, and thirst for the kind of knowledge that leads to financial independence and millionaire status.

In addition, *Figure 13* demonstrates high levels of agreement among millionaires on a vast majority of the 30 statements used in the assessment. Using a standard of 70% to define "agreement," the millionaires found strong common ground on 26 statements. In addition, they found agreement of at least 90% on 19 of the items.

This also takes into account the negatively worded statements for which agreement is defined as less than 30%. For example, only 7% of the millionaires agreed with the statement "I feel pressure to keep up with my friends and family when it comes to money." Researchers expect healthy individuals to "strongly disagree" or "disagree" with that statement, so a 93% disagreement rate is considered positive.

Three additional statements—related to sacrifice, personal goals, and gaining intelligence—garnered at least 50% agreement among the millionaires. Only one statement ("I read approximately one nonfiction book a month") found slightly less than 50% agreement.

Figure 13 Agreement Among Net-Worth Millionaires
(continued on next page)

#	Hypothesis Test With Net-Worth Millionaires	% of Agreement
1	I have a long-term plan for my money	99%
2	My friends and family would describe me as a hard worker	99%
3	I keep my promises and meet my commitments	99%
4	If I start something, I finish it	98%
5	My friends and family would say I am disciplined	98%
6	I do what I think is best, regardless of other people's opinions	98%
7	I accept and integrate feedback from others	98%
8	I almost always achieve my goals	97%
9	I control my own destiny and am responsible for my future	97%
10	I never carry a balance on my credit card	96%
11	I am always trying to learn new things	96%
12	I plan for upcoming expenses by saving in advance	95%
13	I am willing to be wrong and quickly admit to it	95%
14	I live on less money than I make	94%
15	I will try difficult things to get new results	94%
16	I am always trying to improve my habits	94%
17	I feel pressure to keep up with my friends and family when it comes to money	7%
18	I stick to the budgets I create	93%
19	My friends and family would say I am thrifty	90%
20	Challenging myself won't make me any smarter	14%
21	I seek out wisdom from mentors	86%
22	At times, I get jealous of my friends/family because of the things they have or get to do	17%

Figure 13 Agreement Among Net-Worth Millionaires *(continued)*

#	Hypothesis Test With Net-Worth Millionaires	% of Agreement
23	If I am not naturally smart in a subject, I will never do well in it	18%
24	My intelligence is something that I can't change very much	18%
25	With hard work and discipline, anyone can become a millionaire	76%
26	I set aside some of my income every month to give to others	70%
27	There are some things I am not capable of learning	38%
28	I am willing to sacrifice to win—even when it's painful	61%
29	I regularly set personal goals and often write them down	55%
30	I read approximately one nonfiction book a month	45%

Societal Beliefs about Millionaires

General Population Beliefs

In addition to examining the habits and attitudes that led individuals to become millionaires, the research team also wanted to dig deeper into the culture's underlying attitudes toward building wealth. To that end, the team created a list of 10 common beliefs that individuals express about wealthy people and the process of becoming wealthy. They then used a five-point Likert scale to measure the levels of agreement toward each belief within the general population.

Any response that received a majority of agreement (at least 50% of the general population) was considered a belief confirmed. *Figure 14* provides the agreement percentages for each of the 10 beliefs. Of the 10 statements, seven were confirmed by the general population. The most common belief related to the use of debt (86%), followed by the support of wealthy families (77%) and the need to take big risks to make money (67%).

Figure 14 Common Beliefs around Building Wealth

#	Common Beliefs around Building Wealth	General Population
1	Wealthy people use debt in their favor to make more money	86%
2	Most wealthy people come from wealthy families	77%
3	To become rich, you have to take big risks with your money	67%
4	The majority of millionaires inherited their money	62%
5	You need a six-figure salary to become a millionaire in today's economy	62%
6	Most millionaires have a million-dollar home	56%
7	You have to be lucky to get rich	51%
8	Wealthy people are materialistic, self-centered, obsessed with having more	45%
9	To become rich, you need to act rich	25%
10	If you're born into a poor family, you can't become wealthy	18%

Interestingly, two of the three statements that were not confirmed related to general perceptions about wealthy people. The general population essentially denied the beliefs that wealthy people are self-centered (45%) and try to act rich when they are not (25%). The lowest agreement rating was attached to the belief that individuals born into poor families cannot become wealthy (18%).

General Population Compared to Millionaires

When comparing the general population's attitudes toward the responses of millionaires in the study, it becomes apparent that millionaires view the beliefs through a different lens. As *Figure 15b* demonstrates, the millionaires who participated in the research were less likely than the general population to agree with every statement on the list. Nine of the 10 belief statements drew less than 50% affirmation from the Everyday Millionaires in the study.

The differences in responses between millionaires and the general population created substantial gaps for most of the belief statements, as shown in *Figure 15a*. The largest differences between the two groups were found in the beliefs about takings big risks with money (51%) and the value of millionaires' homes (41%). Two other beliefs revealed a difference of at least 30%: Wealthy people come from wealthy families (39%), and most wealthy people inherit their money (31%).

Figure 15a
Differences in Wealth-Building Beliefs between
General Population and Millionaires

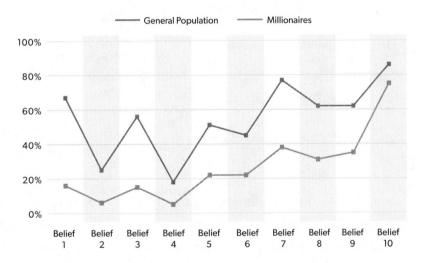

Table 15b Common Beliefs Comparison

Belief #	Common Beliefs and Differences in Agreement	General Population	Millionaires
1	To become rich, you have to take big risks with your money	67%	16%
2	To become rich, you need to act rich	25%	6%
3	Most millionaires have a million-dollar home	56%	15%
4	If you're born into a poor family, you can't become wealthy	18%	5%
5	You have to be lucky to get rich	51%	22%
6	Wealthy people are materialistic, self-centered, obsessed with having more	45%	22%
7	Most wealthy people come from wealthy families	77%	38%
8	The majority of millionaires inherited their money	62%	31%
9	You need a six-figure salary to become a millionaire in today's economy	62%	35%
10	Wealthy people use debt in their favor to make more money	86%	75%

In an interesting note, the lowest margins of disagreement were found on opposite ends of the spectrum. The smallest difference was rooted in the only belief that a majority of millionaires and the general population agreed upon: Using debt as a tool for building wealth (11%). The next smallest margin was found concerning the belief that produced the lowest level of agreement for both groups: Individuals from poor families cannot become millionaires (13%).

Another interesting finding from this data set is the response of Everyday Millionaires to the use of debt in building wealth. As noted above, this was the only belief that drew affirmation from a majority of millionaires in the study (75%). Yet, other parts of the study indicate that most of these millionaires have carefully avoided debt throughout their lives.

Perhaps the best way to reconcile these two perspectives is to consider that while most millionaires have not personally used debt as a tool for building wealth, they may believe that other millionaires have relied on debt to reach their millionaire status.

Generational Beliefs

In addition to making general comparisons between millionaires and the general population, the research team also examined how societal beliefs about wealth played out across various generations. Specifically, the agreement levels for the belief statements were segmented across three broad groupings: Baby Boomers, Generation X, and Millennials. In general, the range of reactions to the common beliefs was more widespread among the younger generations.

Figure 15c Differences in Wealth-Building Beliefs by Generation

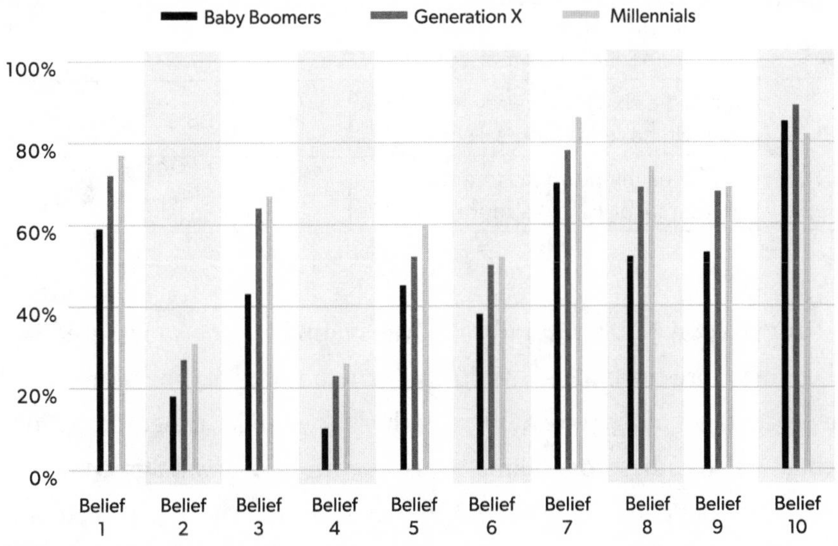

Table 15d Differences in Wealth-Building Beliefs by Generation

Belief #	Common Beliefs around Building Wealth	Boomers	Gen X	Millennials
1	To become rich, you have to take big risks with your money	59%	72%	77%
2	To become rich, you need to act rich	18%	27%	31%
3	Most millionaires have a million-dollar home	43%	64%	67%
4	If you're born into a poor family, you can't become wealthy	10%	23%	26%
5	You have to be lucky to get rich	45%	52%	60%
6	Wealthy people are materialistic, self-centered, obsessed with having more money	38%	50%	52%
7	Most wealthy people come from wealthy families	70%	78%	86%
8	The majority of millionaires inherited their money	52%	69%	74%
9	You need a six-figure salary to become a millionaire in today's economy	53%	68%	69%
10	Wealthy people use debt in their favor to make more money	85%	89%	82%

As the bar graph on *Figure15c* indicates, the common beliefs measured in the study appear to become more entrenched in younger generations. For nine of the 10 belief statements, the percentages of agreement were higher for younger generations. For example, the belief that wealth comes from taking big risks with money was agreed upon by 59% of Baby Boomers, but that percentage was 72% for Generation X and 77% for Millennials. Similarly, while seven in 10 Baby Boomers believe that wealthy people come from wealthy families, the percentages among Generation X (78%) and Millennials (86%) are higher.

Along with this apparent skepticism about what millionaires did to build wealth, younger generations also demonstrated a more negative attitude toward millionaires in general. For instance, only 38% of Baby Boomers think wealthy people are "materialistic, self-centered, and obsessed with having more money." However, that percentage was 50% among members of Generation X and 52% among Millennials. Likewise, Generation X (27%) and Millennials (31%) are more likely to believe that people must act rich to get rich than Baby Boomers in the general population (18%).

The only belief statement that showed variance from this pattern was the final item on the list: "Wealthy people use debt in their favor to make more money." For this statement, 85% of the Baby Boomers in the general population agreed. That number was 89% for Generation X but only 82% for Millennials. *Table 15d* shows the information in numeric form.

Researchers might suggest two explanations (or a combination of them) for these findings. It might be said that younger generations have become more convinced of these beliefs and that they are more cynical than their elders when it comes to building wealth. However, it is also possible that older generations have more experience in building wealth and have discovered that these beliefs are not necessarily accurate. Their experiences make them less likely to affirm the beliefs than younger generations.

Additional Insights from the Research

A random sample of 2,000 net-worth millionaires responded to the 119-question survey instrument as part of *The National Study of Millionaires*. In addition, another 2,000 participants from a random sample of the general population responded to the survey.

This section provides more information and insights into the research results. The six specific areas highlighted in this section include Millionaires and Debt, Millionaires and Saving, Millionaires and Spending, Millionaires and Cars, Millionaires and Building Wealth, and Millionaires and Inheritances.

Millionaires and Debt

The research revealed that millionaires typically avoid debt, especially when compared to the general population. To illustrate this point, **Table 16a** compares the percentages of individuals currently holding debt in both the random sample of 2,000 net-worth millionaires and the random sample drawn from the general population. In almost every category, millionaires are relying on debt much less frequently than non-millionaires.

Table 16a Current Debt Percentages

% Who Currently Hold the Following Debt	General Population	Millionaires
Credit Card Debt	40%	6%
Auto Loan	35%	18%
Student Loan	22%	2%
Medical Debt	12%	2%
Family/Friend Loan	8%	1%
Past-Due Utilities	8%	1%
Cash Advance	4%	1%
Business Loan	2%	2%
Home Equity Loan	9%	10%
Mortgage Loan	34%	30%

For example, 40% of the general population currently have credit card debt, compared to only 6% of millionaires. Likewise, non-millionaires are almost twice as likely to have outstanding car loans (35% compared to 18%) and nearly 10 times more likely to be paying back student loans (22% compared to 2%).

One area in which the percentages for millionaires and the general population are similar is real estate. Millionaires are slightly more likely than non-millionaires to be carrying home equity loans (10% compared to 9%) and almost as likely to have a mortgage (30% for millionaires compared to 34% for the general population). This may be due to the fact that millionaires are more likely to participate in homeownership than non-millionaires. Also, it should be noted that unlike consumer debt, real estate tends to rise in value over time, making a mortgage less dangerous than other forms of debt.

Some might argue that millionaires inherently have less need of debt than members of the general population. Because they have attained financial independence, they do not have to rely on debt instruments, such as loans and credit cards. However, **Table 16b** indicates that, in general, millionaires have always avoided debt throughout the course of their lives—even before they became millionaires.

Table 16b Lifetime Debt Percentages

% Who Have *Ever* Held the Following Debt	General Population	Millionaires
Credit Card Debt	66%	27%
Student Loan	47%	29%
Family/Friend Loan	37%	19%
Past-Due Utilities	29%	4%
Cash Advance	17%	6%
Medical Debt	35%	7%
Auto Loan	73%	65%
Business Loan	8%	10%
Home Equity Loan	28%	37%
Mortgage Loan	62%	86%

For example, millionaires are more than twice as likely to have stayed away from credit card debt than the general population over time. Nearly three-fourths of all millionaires (73%) said they have *never* had credit card debt. Meanwhile, only 34% of the general population could say the same.

Likewise, only 4% of millionaires said they have ever paid a utility bill late, compared to almost one-third (29%) of the general population. And while nearly one-half of non-millionaires have taken out student loans (47%), less than a third of millionaires (29%) ever borrowed money to pay for college.

Again, the percentage of millionaires who have held home equity loans or mortgages is higher than the general population. But, as noted, this might be attributed to the number of millionaires who actually own their homes compared to non-millionaires.

Figure 16c Millionaires and Debt (Full Data)

Which of these debts do you hold today or have you held in the past?

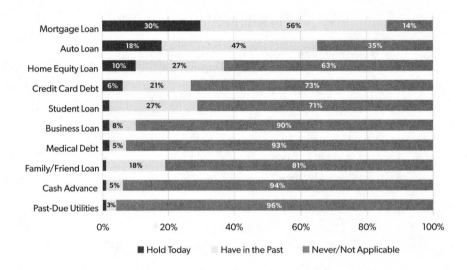

Figure 16d General Population and Debt (Full Data)

Which of these debts do you hold today or have you held in the past?

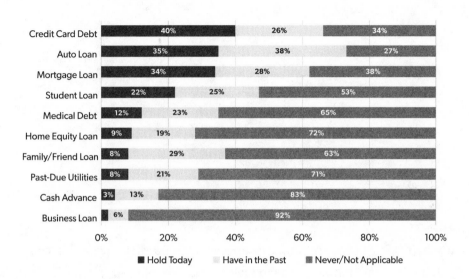

Millionaires and Saving

As noted earlier, most Everyday Millionaires surveyed in *The National Study of Millionaires* did not inherit the bulk of their wealth. Any money they may have received from their families was not enough to establish a million-dollar net worth. In fact, many essentially built their wealth from scratch after being raised in low- to moderate-income families.

This being the case, it is reasonable to assume that at some point in life these millionaires learned the value of saving money. The research indicates that this includes applying discipline to set money aside for the future through savings accounts or investment tools. But it also involves saving money in the present through budgeting and other habits.

Saving for the Future. In general, millionaires can be classified as "savers." The Everyday Millionaires who took part in *The National Study of Millionaires* follow that pattern in their own lives. As shown in ***Figure 17a***, only 3% of the millionaires in the research reported that they set nothing aside in savings each month.

Figure 17a Millionaires and Percentage of Income Saved per Month

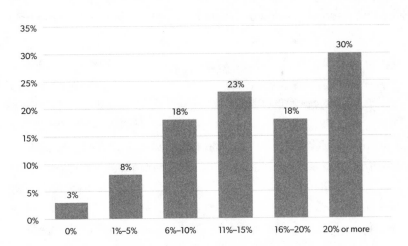

Nearly half (48%) of the millionaires questioned said they save at least 16% of their income each month, including 30% who save at least 20% of their income. In fact, almost nine out of 10 participants (89%) set aside at least 6% each month.

These numbers suggest at least two important implications for millionaires. First, such commitment to saving underscores the importance of regular saving as a tool for reaching millionaire status. Saving money not only provides security in the present through the presence of an emergency fund, but it also primes the pump for investments that build wealth over time. Setting aside money not only increases the principal for investments, but it also positively impacts the overall return, regardless of the interest rate. So, while the old cliché says one must spend money to make money, a better understanding from the examples of millionaires is that one must *save* money to make money.

Second, the pattern of millionaires debunks the myth that ordinary people do not make enough money to save. The research indicates that the individuals in the study began saving long before reaching millionaire status and have carried that habit with them through time. One-third of the participants in the study never had a six-figure household income. In fact, the top three professions listed in the survey were engineer, accountant, and teacher. So, these Everyday Millionaires did not build wealth by earning a large salary. Instead, millionaires create a plan and exercise the discipline to stick with that plan. Their ability to save up to double-digit percentages of their monthly income suggests that anyone can follow that example.

Saving in the Present. The research team discovered that Everyday Millionaires are not beyond hunting for bargains whenever possible. For example, **Figure 17b** found that more than one in three millionaires in the study said they use coupons "all the time." Another 58% use them "some of the time." Only 7% never use coupons to save money on their purchases.

Figure 17b Frequency of Millionaires' Coupon Usage

All the time	35%
Some of the time	58%
Never	7%

0%   20%   40%   60%

Figure 17c Millionaires Have Shopped at Thrift Stores in the Past 12 Months

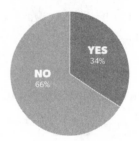

YES 34%

NO 66%

Likewise, **Figure 17c** reveals that approximately one-third of these millionaires state that they have shopped at a thrift store of some kind in the last 12 months. While the research does not indicate the kind of purchases they made, it is worth noting that so many individuals living at millionaire status have opted for secondhand clothing or other items recently.

Millionaires also used one other common tool for saving money: a shopping list. **Figure 17d** shows that many millionaires rely on a list at least some of the time when they go to the grocery store. According to the responses from the study, more than a quarter of Everyday Millionaires (28%) make and stick to a shopping list. Another 57% make a list and "somewhat stick to it." So, 85% of participants in *The National Study of Millionaires* relied on a grocery list to some degree.

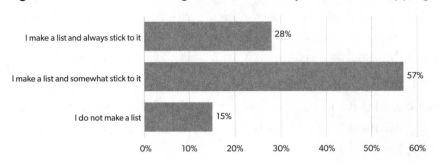

Figure 17d Millionaires Using a Written Grocery List When Shopping

Based on the research, it seems that a substantial number of millionaires have not completely abandoned many of the frugal habits they learned early in their wealth-building journey. Even though their financial situation has expanded, they still take advantage of their old habits to continue building wealth. This is another indication that millionaires do not always act like the stereotypes so often applied to them.

Millionaires and Spending

The research examined the spending habits of millionaires from several different perspectives. But three of the most interesting areas of study were shopping for groceries, eating at restaurants, and buying clothes.

GROCERIES. Based on the research, the average millionaire in this study spends approximately $412 each month on groceries as a group. Meanwhile, one report from the USDA states that a comparable family in the general population spends more than $582 a month on groceries.[4] So, in general, it can be said that millionaires are more frugal than non-millionaires in their approach to grocery shopping.

Figure 18 breaks down how much the millionaires in the study said they spend each month on groceries. More than one-third (36%) spend less than $300 each month and

---

[4] United States Department of Agriculture, "Official USDA Food Plans: Cost of Food at Home at Four Levels, U.S. Average," March 2017.

almost two-thirds (64%) spend less than $450. Less than one in five (19%) spends more than $600 on groceries.

Figure 18 Millionaires' Monthly Grocery Expenditures

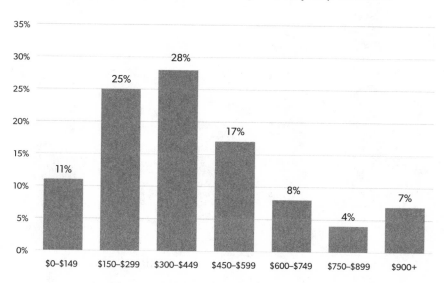

RESTAURANTS. If many millionaires limit the amount of money they spend on groceries, it is fair to wonder if they compensate by spending more at restaurants. The study results indicate that they do not. The median millionaire in this study stated that they spend less than $200 each month at restaurants. Meanwhile, the Bureau of Labor Statistics reports that the median American household spends approximately $251 eating out each month.[5]

Figure 19 demonstrates that roughly two-thirds of millionaires spend less than $300 at restaurants each month, with 36% spending less than $150. Only 17% spend more than $450 a month, dispelling the image of a stereotypical millionaire eating out at extravagant restaurants every night. The research shows that a vast majority of millionaires are much more frugal than their general population counterparts.

---

[5] U.S. Bureau of Labor Statistics, "Consumer Expenditures in 2015," April 2017.

Figure 19 Millionaires' Monthly Restaurant Expenditures

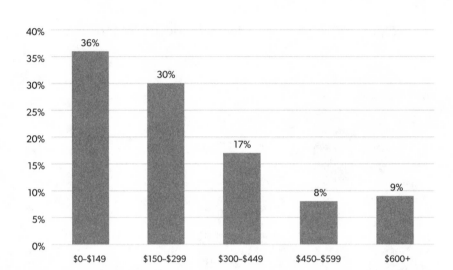

CLOTHING. Another cultural stereotype involves wealthy individuals who spend large sums of money on expensive clothes. Again, the responses provided for *The National Study of Millionaires* demonstrate that this stereotype is a myth. The millionaires included in this research reported that they spend an average of $117 a month on clothes, while the Bureau of Labor Statistics reports that the average American household spends $154 a month.[6]

Figure 20 reveals that more than three-fourths of the millionaires in the study's random sample spend less than $150 each month on clothes. Only one in five of these individuals spend more than $200. So, as with groceries and restaurants, millionaires appear to be more frugal in their clothing budgets than members of the general population.

---

[6] U.S. Bureau of Labor Statistics, "Consumer Expenditures in 2015," April 2017.

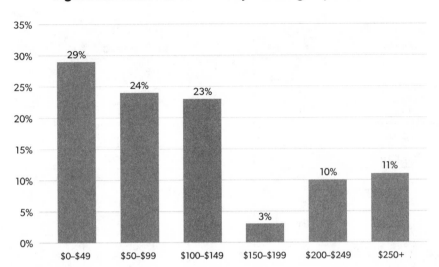

Figure 20 Millionaires' Monthly Clothing Expenditures

Millionaires and Cars

To determine if millionaires display their wealth through the cars they drive, the survey instrument asked participants to share information about their automobiles. The results affirmed the basic hypothesis that millionaires primarily avoid "luxury" vehicles.

Table 21 provides a percentage ranking of the automobiles driven by the millionaires in the study. The two most popular makes of cars were Toyota and Honda, with nearly one-third of all millionaires (31%) identifying one of those brands. The top American brand was Ford, placing third on the list and tying Lexus (the first luxury model mentioned) at only 8%.

While three luxury models were included in the millionaires' top 10 list, the percentages for those automobiles were relatively low. As noted, Lexus scored highest at 8%. Meanwhile, BMW and Acura accounted for only 4% and 3%, respectively. Combined, the top three luxury models garnered just 15% of the total.

These results indicate that the millionaires in this study did not necessarily favor expensive, luxury cars. As with the other categories mentioned, "frugality" is an apt descriptor of their approach to vehicles.

Table 21 Top 20 Brands of Millionaires' Cars

Car Brands of Millionaires	Market Share	Car Brands of Millionaires	Market Share
Toyota	16%	Mercedes	3%
Honda	15%	Chevrolet	3%
Ford	8%	Nissan	3%
Lexus	8%	Audi	3%
Subaru	5%	Cadillac	2%
BMW	4%	Volvo	2%
Acura	3%	Mazda	2%
Hyundai	3%	Jeep	2%
Lincoln	3%	Dodge	2%
Buick	3%	Chrysler	2%

Millionaires and Building Wealth

Under the topic "Millionaires' Net Worth," this report considered the factors that millionaires in the study believe are important for building wealth. But this portion of the report examines the actual tools that they used to build their wealth.

The millionaires in the study were asked to share which tools they used to build their seven-figure net worth. ***Table 22a*** shares the percentages for the top six responses. Far and away, the millionaires view investing as the primary tool for building wealth and securing financial independence.

Eight out of 10 millionaires in the study (80%) listed investing in their employer-sponsored retirement plan as a primary vehicle for reaching that status. Meanwhile, 74% mentioned investing outside the company plan, and 73% mentioned the habit of saving money regularly.

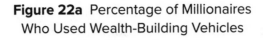

Figure 22a Percentage of Millionaires
Who Used Wealth-Building Vehicles

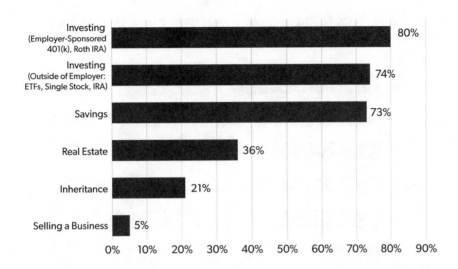

The importance of a company's retirement plan was not an unexpected response for the researchers. Most employer-sponsored plans are tax-favored or tax-free. They also tend to include some level of a company match that provides employees with "free" money for investing. Likewise, because most employer-sponsored plans have government-imposed annual contribution limits, it also makes sense that millionaires look for additional investing options outside of their company plan. And while the interest earned on typical savings accounts do not provide the yield of other investments, they are still reliable and safe tools for growing a margin of wealth.

After selecting which tools were used in creating financial independence, the millionaires were asked to rank each tool in order of importance. Engagement with wealth-building vehicles was critical to know, but understanding which ones had the most influence in reaching seven-figure net worth was vital. To ensure accuracy, study participants were asked which vehicles they used for building wealth and, on a later question, were shown only those items to rank by importance. This method allowed the research team to eliminate items that were not relevant to the process of building wealth and to create a set of weighted ratings for each tool. The result of those weighted ratings was an "Importance Score" for each tool, as demonstrated in *Figure 22b*.

Figure 22b Rank Distribution and Importance Scores of Millionaires' Vehicles Used to Build Wealth

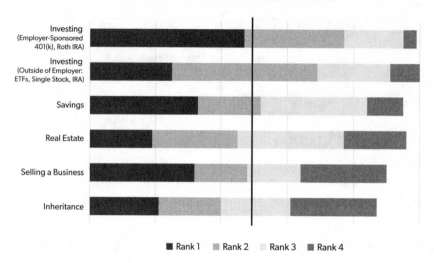

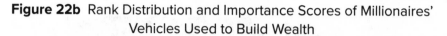

Table 22c Rank Distribution and Importance Scores of Millionaires' Vehicles Used to Build Wealth

Rank Distribution	1	2	3	4	Importance Score
Investing (Employer)	47%	30%	18%	4%	6.17
Investing (Outside of Employer)	25%	44%	22%	9%	5.84
Savings	33%	19%	32%	11%	5.68
Real Estate	19%	26%	32%	19%	5.38
Selling a Business	32%	16%	16%	26%	5.32
Inheritance	21%	19%	21%	26%	5.05

For the importance score, responses were weighted so that items ranked first were given greater weight. The score, computed for each answer option/row header, is the sum of all weighted values. The weighted values were then determined by the number of columns included.

As **Table 22c** indicates, 47% of millionaires in the study ranked the employer-sponsored retirement plan first, while another 30% ranked it second. As a result, this tool ended up with the largest importance factor on the list at 6.17. When combined with information from **Figure 22a**, the research indicates that a vast majority of millionaires used a company plan to build wealth and believe it is *the primary tool* for reaching financial independence. Likewise, the millionaires also see the importance of investing outside of the company. Nearly two-thirds of respondents ranked this as either first or second, which produced a weighted importance score of 5.84. In the research interviews, millionaires mentioned taking advantage of IRAs and ETFs (specifically low-cost index funds) as some of the keys to growing their wealth.

Two tools that do not appear to be high priorities for the millionaires are selling a business and receiving an inheritance. Less than half of millionaires who sold businesses (48%) ranked this in the top two on their lists and earned an importance score of only 5.32. This was somewhat surprising, because one might assume that the sale of a company would produce a sizable windfall. This may be related to the types of businesses being sold—small businesses, such as landscaping companies or home appraisal services. It's unlikely that type of sale would net millions in profit—perhaps a few hundred thousand—thereby leading the owner to rely on additional avenues of building wealth.

Likewise, inheritances ranked at the bottom of the millionaires' list with an importance score of 5.05. Only one in five millionaires who received an inheritance placed it first in their rankings.

The next section of the research provides some explanation as to why the millionaires in this study downplayed the role of inheritances in their efforts to build wealth.

Millionaires and Inheritances

As noted above, the research identified a discrepancy between how the millionaires viewed the role of inheritances in building wealth and how the general population perceived inheritances. In general, the millionaires downplayed the importance of inheritances, while non-millionaires considered them second only to financial discipline in a list of factors that contribute to millionaire status. In addition, only 4% of millionaires in the study ranked it first in terms of tools used for building wealth, producing the lowest importance score at 5.05.

A deeper dive into the research demonstrates that the millionaires' own experiences could explain why they see inheritances differently than the general population. *Figure 23* reveals that 79% of all millionaires in the study have never received an inheritance. It should be noted that 21% did receive an inheritance, which roughly aligns with what government data from the U.S. Bureau of Labor Statistics has found in the general population.[7] Millionaires are no more likely to receive an inheritance than the average American.

It is safe to say very few of these individuals relied on inherited money to build their financial independence. Of those who received an inheritance, few received a large enough inheritance to actually move the needle in their financial lives. Approximately half of these individuals were given less than $250,000. While this would certainly help in one's journey toward a seven-figure net worth, it typically is not enough to push a portfolio over the top. Other investments and savings are necessary for an individual to become a millionaire.

---

[7] U.S. Bureau of Labor Statistics, "Inheritances and the Distribution of Wealth or Whatever Happened to the Great Inheritance Boom?," January 2011.

Figure 23 Millionaires and Inheritances Received

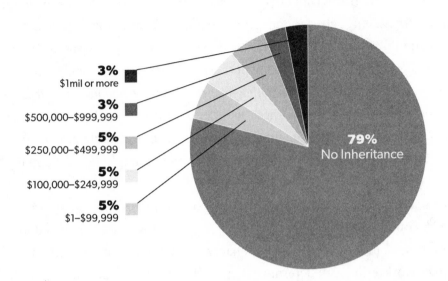

3%
$1mil or more

3%
$500,000–$999,999

5%
$250,000–$499,999

5%
$100,000–$249,999

5%
$1–$99,999

79%
No Inheritance

Even adding the next level of the pie chart into the equation does not significantly change the impact of inheritances on an individual's ability to reach millionaire status. As stated, approximately one in nine millionaires received less than $250,000. Adding the next sliver indicates that 94% of all millionaires in the study received less than $500,000. Again, this is undeniably a large number, but it is not the sole factor in these individuals becoming millionaires.

According to this research, only 3% of the respondents received an inheritance of at least $1 million—essentially securing millionaire status. The vast majority of them built wealth through other tools, such as employer-sponsored retirement plans and other investments outside of a company plan.

Conclusion

The Ramsey Solutions research team set out to conduct the largest study of millionaires ever. Between the qualitative and quantitative phases of the research, this effort included the responses of more than 10,000 millionaires, including a statistically significant random sample of 2,000 millionaires with no prior connection to Ramsey Solutions. It also provided comparison criteria through a random general population sampling of 2,000 individuals.

As stated in this paper's introduction, the purpose of the study was to determine the validity of the following alternative hypothesis: *Millionaires gain wealth through specific choices, such as working hard, demonstrating financial discipline, and investing consistently and wisely over time.* This working hypothesis would not only identify key characteristics that individuals can use in finding financial independence, but it would also debunk several myths and misunderstandings about building wealth that might be common in the general population.

After analyzing the results of this extensive study, the research team can assert with a degree of confidence that the alternative hypothesis was validated. Over and over and in multiple ways, millionaires stated a reliance on elements within their control—such as positive work ethic, self-determination, and personal responsibility—rather than elements they could not control—such as luck, socioeconomic upbringing, or large inheritances—to gain their millionaire status and their financial independence.

Among the insights gained from the research:

- Millionaires generally steer clear of debt in any form. For example, almost three-quarters of millionaires in the study had never had either credit card debt (73%) or student loan debt (71%). More than nine in 10 have never even paid a utility bill late.
- Millionaires tend to demonstrate a "growth mindset" rather than a "fixed mindset"—a mentality of abundance rather than scarcity. They embrace change and usually see adversity as an opportunity for growth. Perseverance is a key quality for millionaires.
- Millionaires tend to be frugal—not flashy. Instead of diving into extravagance, the millionaires in the study spend less than the general population on groceries, restaurants, and clothing. Most also drive moderately priced cars and live in

houses that are smaller than the national average. More than half live in neighborhoods where the average household income is less than $75,000 a year.

- Millionaires consider financial discipline and consistent investing as the primary tools for building financial independence. The most important priorities for the millionaires in this study include the following: taking advantage of employer-provided retirement plans, investing outside of company plans, and saving in other areas.

- Millionaires generally downplay the importance of luck and inheritances. Since they emphasize things they can control, they do not believe luck has had an impact on their financial success. And because only one in five millionaires in the study has received an inheritance, it does not represent a reliable tool in building wealth.

- Millionaires believe that virtually anyone can follow their path and become a millionaire. The millionaires in the study do not believe wealth building is a quick or easy process. It has taken most of them decades to reach a seven-figure net worth. But they demonstrate a confidence that anyone can reach this milestone through discipline and hard work over time.

The depth of this research has yielded a vast quantity of reliable information and insights related to the mindset and behaviors of "everyday" millionaires that could open doors for additional research in this field in the years to come. While this white paper includes deeper dives into several areas of *The National Study of Millionaires* research, even more information is included in the attached appendix. This could provide interested parties with even more data for comparison and further study.

However, it should be emphasized that this paper—along with the research upon which it is based—is not designed solely to outline academic theory. *The National Study of Millionaires* also contains practical suggestions for individuals who might strive to reach millionaire status. It holds the key to creating financial independence, which can make a difference for countless families and their communities.

Appendix

The following section of the report contains tables and cross tabulations on various topics from *The National Study of Millionaires*. The raw data allows one to study the numbers and draw conclusions not included in the white paper.

APPENDIX A

The Mean Age at Which
Millionaire Status Was Achieved, by Cohort

Millionaire Status Achieved	Average Age
Overall Age	50
By Birth Order	
First	50
Middle	51
Youngest	48
Only	47
By Type of Student	
A Student	49
B Student	51
C Student	50
By Type of College	
Public	50
Private	49
Ivy League	48
Community	52
By Education Level	
No degree	53
Bachelor's	50
Graduate	48
Terminal	50
By Upbringing	
Lower Class	50
Lower-Middle Class	51
Middle Class	51
Upper-Middle Class	46
Upper Class	36

By Books Read per Year	
0	50
1–5	50
6–10	50
11 or More	48
By Budget Frequency	
Rarely/Never	50
Some Months	48
Most Months	47

APPENDIX B

The Median and Average Net Worth
of Study Participants, by Cohort

Net Worth	Median	Average
Overall Net Worth	$2,485,000	$3,544,535
By Region		
Northeast	$2,677,400	$3,774,181
Midwest	$2,202,500	$3,093,377
South	$2,340,000	$3,499,407
West	$2,500,000	$3,745,194
By Area		
Urban	$2,750,000	$4,051,116
Suburban	$2,500,000	$3,492,133
Rural	$2,057,500	$3,188,598
By Birth Order		
First	$2,500,000	$3,694,564
Middle	$2,100,000	$2,974,581
Youngest	$2,500,000	$3,625,068
Only	$2,817,500	$3,864,104
By Type of Student		
A Student	$2,500,000	$3,716,774
B Student	$2,397,000	$3,014,225
C Student	$2,500,000	$4,509,344
By Type of College		
Public	$2,340,000	$3,430,463
Private	$2,494,000	$3,847,615
Ivy League	$3,330,000	$5,096,412
Community	$2,000,000	$2,694,575
By Education Level		
No degree	$2,600,000	$3,047,317
Bachelor's	$2,250,000	$3,135,537

APPENDIX

Net Worth	Median	Average
Graduate	$2,465,000	$3,519,799
Terminal	$3,400,000	$5,353,543
By Upbringing		
Lower Class	$2,440,000	$2,965,184
Lower-Middle Class	$2,485,000	$3,149,763
Middle Class	$2,300,000	$3,538,370
Upper-Middle Class	$2,625,000	$3,765,220
Upper Class	$6,000,000	$13,202,222
Overall Net Worth	$2,485,000	$3,544,535
By Books Read Per Year		
0	$2,350,000	$3,785,843
1–5	$2,380,000	$3,388,329
6–10	$2,500,000	$3,229,825
11 or More	$2,500,000	$3,953,158
By Personality		
Introvert	$2,300,000	$3,396,074
Extrovert	$2,500,000	$3,718,052
By Relationship Status		
Married	$2,500,000	$3,539,520
Single	$2,300,000	$3,218,905
Divorced	$2,375,000	$3,033,821
By Career Satisfaction		
Love my work	$2,500,000	$3,800,549
Neutral about my work	$2,163,000	$3,193,973
I do not like my work	$1,900,000	$2,400,568

APPENDIX C

*Ownership of Primary Residence, Estimated Home Value
and Square Footage, by Cohort*

Primary Residence	Paid-For Residence	Median Home Value	Average Value	Median Square Footage	Average Square Footage
Overall	68%	$450,000	$631,364	2,500	2,638
By Region					
Northeast	74%	$500,000	$680,995	2,500	2,607
Midwest	69%	$325,000	$403,046	2,500	2,741
South	68%	$412,500	$530,647	2,600	2,793
West	63%	$650,000	$892,438	2,300	2,422
By Area					
Urban	67%	$550,000	$753,519	2,000	2,266
Suburban	67%	$450,000	$632,832	2,500	2,746
Rural	75%	$385,000	$493,487	2,400	2,621
By Household Size					
1	72%	$375,000	$590,959	1,990	2,081
2	73%	$450,000	$596,052	2,500	2,627
3	62%	$550,000	$902,034	3,000	2,943
4	39%	$455,000	$653,346	2,800	3,040
5 or More	48%	$520,000	$588,864	2,950	3,235
By Net Worth					
$1mil–$1.99mil	56%	$375,000	$446,681	2,300	2,378
$2mil–$2.99mil	76%	$400,000	$498,500	2,400	2,562
$3mil–$3.99mil	74%	$500,000	$616,374	2,500	2,646
$4mil–$4.99mil	76%	$650,000	$781,657	2,500	2,789
$5mil+	76%	$750,000	$1,137,933	3,200	3,360

By Age					
Under 45	36%	$540,000	$685,930	2,450	2,711
45–54	49%	$450,000	$810,622	2,500	2,790
55–64	65%	$410,000	$545,648	2,500	2,623
65–74	75%	$450,000	$566,470	2,500	2,654
75 or Older	92%	$482,500	$639,035	2,300	2,466
By Upbringing					
Lower Class	68%	$492,500	$540,250	2,600	2,772
Lower-Middle Class	73%	$425,000	$553,938	2,400	2,552
Middle Class	69%	$425,000	$625,925	2,400	2,575
Upper-Middle Class	60%	$537,500	$763,651	2,800	2,840
Upper Class	57%	$600,000	$974,333	3,600	3,444

APPENDIX D

Type of Primary Residence, by Cohort
(not all cohorts add to 100 due to senior-living facilities,
living with family, etc.)

Type of Primary Residence	House	Town House/ Condo	Apartment
Overall	82%	13%	4%
By Region			
Northeast	76%	14%	8%
Midwest	88%	10%	2%
South	81%	15%	3%
West	84%	11%	4%
By Area			
Urban	62%	24%	13%
Suburban	86%	11%	2%
Rural	91%	5%	2%
By Household Size			
1	57%	29%	14%
2	84%	12%	3%
3	94%	4%	2%
4	97%	0%	1%
5 or More	100%	0%	0%
By Net Worth			
$1mil–$1.99mil	82%	13%	4%
$2mil–$2.99mil	81%	13%	5%
$3mil–$3.99mil	85%	11%	2%
$4mil–$4.99mil	85%	11%	5%
$5mil+	75%	16%	7%

APPENDIX

By Age			
Under 45	76%	11%	11%
45–54	87%	7%	5%
55–64	85%	12%	2%
65–74	81%	14%	4%
75 or Older	74%	11%	5%
By Upbringing			
Lower Class	86%	7%	5%
Lower-Middle Class	84%	11%	3%
Middle Class	82%	13%	5%
Upper-Middle Class	76%	17%	6%
Upper Class	86%	9%	5%

APPENDIX E

Years to Pay Off Primary Residence, by Cohort

Years to Pay Off Primary Residence	Average
Overall	10.2 years
By Region	
Northeast	10.9
Midwest	10.4
South	8.4
West	11.7
By Area	
Urban	10.1
Suburban	11.3
Rural	6.9
By Net Worth	
$1mil–$1.99mil	12
$2mil–$2.99mil	9.7
$3mil–$3.99mil	10.3
$4mil–$4.99mil	9.1
$5mil+	7.9
By Years to Become Millionaire	
10 or Less	5.9
11–20	7.2
21–30	10.0
31–40	12.1
40+	12.7

By Upbringing	
Lower Class	9.6
Lower-Middle Class	10.7
Middle Class	10.2
Upper-Middle Class	10.1
Upper Class	8.9

APPENDIX F

Monthly Grocery Expenditure, by Cohort

Monthly Grocery Expenditure	Average
Overall Expenditure	$412
By Region	
Northeast	$414
Midwest	$405
South	$401
West	$429
By Area	
Urban	$392
Suburban	$416
Rural	$408
By Household Size	
1	$231
2	$408
3	$513
4	$538
5 or More	$561
By Net Worth	
$1mil–$1.99mil	$417
$2mil–$2.99mil	$390
$3mil–$3.99mil	$361
$4mil–$4.99mil	$388
$5mil+	$505
By Employment Status	
Working	$424
Retired	$373

By Age	
Under 45	$421
45–54	$487
55–64	$426
65–74	$379
75 or Older	$364

APPENDIX G

Monthly Restaurant Expenditure, by Cohort

Monthly Restaurant Expenditure	Average
Overall Expenditure	$267
By Region	
Northeast	$292
Midwest	$279
South	$256
West	$250
By Area	
Urban	$290
Suburban	$277
Rural	$179
By Household Size	
1	$185
2	$278
3	$246
4	$322
5 or More	$296
By Budget Frequency	
Rarely/Never	$270
Some Months	$292
Most Months	$214
By Net Worth	
$1mil–$1.99mil	$250
$2mil–$2.99mil	$226
$3mil–$3.99mil	$310
$4mil–$4.99mil	$262
$5mil+	$320

By Employment Status	
Working	$282
Retired	$245
By Coupon Usage	
Use Coupons	$222
Don't Use Coupons	$345
By Personality	
Introvert	$234
Extrovert	$304

APPENDIX H

Monthly Clothing Expenditure, by Cohort

Monthly Clothing Expenditure	Average Expenditure
Overall Expenditure	$117
By Region	
Northeast	$114
Midwest	$133
South	$115
West	$113
By Area	
Urban	$134
Suburban	$123
Rural	$70
By Household Size	
1	$108
2	$103
3	$135
4	$178
5 or More	$186
By Net Worth	
$1mil–$1.99mil	$100
$2mil–$2.99mil	$95
$3mil–$3.99mil	$112
$4mil–$4.99mil	$123
$5mil+	$165
By Employment Status	
Working	$136
Retired	$84

By Age	
Under 45	$244
45–54	$151
55–64	$118
65–74	$94
75 or Older	$82

APPENDIX I

Vehicles Used to Build Wealth, by Cohort

Building Wealth	Investing (Company)	Investing (Individual)	Real Estate	Inheritance	Selling a Business	Income to Savings (More Than 15%)	Used Financial Planner
Overall	80%	74%	36%	21%	5%	48%	68%
By Region							
Northeast	78%	74%	33%	22%	5%	45%	67%
Midwest	83%	75%	27%	20%	5%	52%	71%
South	82%	75%	36%	20%	4%	49%	65%
West	75%	73%	44%	20%	6%	44%	70%
By Area							
Urban	74%	75%	40%	23%	3%	49%	67%
Suburban	81%	73%	34%	19%	5%	47%	69%
Rural	84%	78%	34%	23%	6%	47%	69%
By Age							
Under 45	70%	62%	41%	8%	3%	54%	59%
45–54	76%	73%	32%	14%	3%	59%	63%
55–64	84%	71%	30%	16%	6%	57%	65%
65–74	84%	79%	41%	25%	4%	41%	71%
75 or Older	75%	77%	38%	30%	7%	32%	75%
By Net Worth							
$1mil–$1.99mil	84%	74%	34%	22%	5%	43%	69%
$2mil–$2.99mil	84%	81%	31%	18%	2%	48%	67%
$3mil–$3.99mil	82%	78%	39%	20%	6%	46%	69%
$4mil–$4.99mil	80%	82%	39%	25%	5%	57%	67%
$5mil+	72%	71%	48%	25%	9%	55%	66%

By Upbringing							
Lower Class	79%	81%	42%	14%	2%	58%	67%
Lower-Middle Class	82%	78%	35%	19%	5%	45%	65%
Middle Class	82%	75%	36%	21%	5%	49%	69%
Upper-Middle Class	72%	67%	34%	25%	5%	45%	69%
Upper Class	64%	55%	45%	14%	0%	41%	91%
Overall	80%	74%	36%	21%	5%	48%	68%
By Education Level							
No degree	67%	74%	36%	14%	8%	52%	64%
Bachelor's	78%	73%	35%	21%	5%	46%	70%
Graduate	82%	76%	32%	21%	4%	47%	68%
Terminal	82%	74%	40%	24%	3%	49%	72%
By Type of College							
Public	82%	74%	35%	21%	4%	49%	67%
Private	81%	76%	34%	21%	4%	48%	70%
Ivy League	81%	77%	44%	28%	3%	33%	71%
Community	87%	79%	39%	23%	9%	57%	72%
By Books Read per Year							
0	80%	71%	34%	15%	4%	57%	59%
1–5	77%	72%	36%	21%	5%	44%	72%
6–10	83%	77%	34%	22%	6%	40%	69%
11 or More	83%	81%	37%	23%	4%	52%	70%
By Years to Become Millionaire							
10 or Less	55%	68%	55%	18%	5%	48%	50%
11–20	80%	77%	34%	11%	5%	64%	63%
21–30	82%	79%	37%	14%	4%	53%	62%
31–40	84%	73%	33%	29%	4%	39%	74%
40+	81%	77%	36%	42%	2%	33%	77%

APPENDIX J

Common Beliefs in General Population, by Cohort

General Population	Belief 1	Belief 2	Belief 3	Belief 4	Belief 5
Overall	86%	77%	67%	62%	62%
By Region					
Northeast	82%	81%	74%	65%	67%
Midwest	87%	79%	63%	63%	58%
South	84%	69%	66%	60%	59%
West	87%	80%	73%	69%	64%
By Area					
Urban	85%	76%	69%	64%	62%
Rural	90%	81%	60%	56%	62%
By Generation					
Baby Boomer	85%	70%	59%	52%	53%
Generation X	89%	78%	72%	69%	68%
Millennials	82%	86%	77%	74%	69%
By Education Level					
No Degree	93%	86%	58%	59%	47%
Bachelor's	85%	74%	64%	55%	57%
Graduate	86%	77%	64%	58%	59%
Terminal	85%	76%	73%	71%	71%

BELIEF 1
Wealthy people use debt in their favor to make more money.

BELIEF 2
Most wealthy people come from wealthy families.

BELIEF 3
To become rich, you have to take big risks with your money.

By Upbringing					
Lower Class	84%	74%	77%	66%	67%
Lower-Middle Class	87%	77%	69%	63%	64%
Middle Class	86%	78%	68%	62%	60%
Upper-Middle Class	86%	77%	58%	62%	60%
Upper Class	74%	71%	67%	76%	56%
By Type of College					
Public	89%	78%	67%	60%	59%
Private	82%	76%	61%	59%	56%
Ivy League	92%	83%	60%	56%	54%
Community	83%	80%	70%	70%	61%
By Outlook					
Optimist	87%	75%	69%	62%	60%
Pessimist	81%	84%	63%	66%	66%

BELIEF 4
The majority of millionaires inherited their money.

BELIEF 5
You need a six-figure salary to become a millionaire in today's economy.

APPENDIX J *(continued)*

Common Beliefs in General Population, by Cohort

General Population	Belief 6	Belief 7	Belief 8	Belief 9	Belief 10
Overall	56%	51%	45%	25%	18%
By Region					
Northeast	63%	60%	53%	26%	21%
Midwest	53%	50%	43%	21%	15%
South	51%	45%	42%	25%	17%
West	61%	53%	45%	30%	18%
By Area					
Urban	57%	52%	45%	26%	18%
Rural	53%	48%	46%	19%	17%
By Generation					
Baby Boomer	43%	45%	38%	18%	10%
Generation X	64%	52%	50%	27%	23%
Millennials	67%	60%	52%	31%	26%
By Education Level					
No Degree	40%	58%	44%	29%	18%
Bachelor's	50%	44%	37%	18%	13%
Graduate	52%	50%	41%	27%	20%
Terminal	66%	55%	54%	26%	20%

BELIEF 6
Most millionaires have a million-dollar home.

BELIEF 7
You have to be lucky to get rich.

BELIEF 8
Wealthy people are materialistic, self-centered, and obsessed with having more.

By Upbringing					
Lower Class	58%	57%	59%	20%	24%
Lower-Middle Class	57%	50%	44%	20%	14%
Middle Class	57%	50%	44%	26%	18%
Upper-Middle Class	48%	52%	41%	27%	16%
Upper Class	63%	68%	50%	60%	53%
By Type of College					
Public	54%	52%	41%	27%	16%
Private	44%	48%	38%	17%	14%
Ivy League	64%	67%	45%	33%	33%
Community	56%	43%	41%	20%	17%
By Outlook					
Optimist	56%	48%	43%	25%	17%
Pessimist	57%	58%	50%	24%	21%

BELIEF 9
To become rich, you need to act rich.

BELIEF 10
If you're born into a poor family, you can't become wealthy.

APPENDIX K
*Becoming a Millionaire Is More about Personal Habits
or External Circumstances, by Cohort*

Becoming a Millionaire Is More About . . .	Personal Habits	External Circumstances
Overall	84%	16%
By Region		
Northeast	81%	19%
Midwest	87%	13%
South	84%	16%
West	86%	14%
By Area		
Urban	77%	23%
Suburban	87%	13%
Rural	86%	14%
By Upbringing		
Lower Class	84%	16%
Lower-Middle Class	87%	13%
Middle Class	85%	15%
Upper-Middle Class	79%	21%
Upper Class	83%	17%
By Net Worth		
$1mil–$1.99mil	87%	13%
$2mil–$2.99mil	85%	15%
$3mil–$3.99mil	80%	20%
$4mil–$4.99mil	83%	17%
$5mil+	87%	13%

By Years to Become Millionaire		
10 or Less	76%	24%
11–20	86%	14%
21–30	88%	12%
31–40	84%	16%
40+	80%	20%
By Birth Order		
First	82%	18%
Middle	88%	12%
Youngest	88%	12%
Only	79%	21%
Overall	84%	16%
By Type of Student		
A Student	82%	18%
B Student	88%	12%
C Student	88%	12%
By Type of College		
Public	84%	16%
Private	83%	17%
Ivy League	80%	20%
Community	88%	12%
By Education Level		
No Degree	89%	11%
Bachelor's	88%	12%
Graduate	83%	17%
Terminal	74%	26%

By Books Read per Year		
0	87%	13%
1–5	84%	16%
6–10	85%	15%
11 or More	81%	19%
By Age		
Under 45	75%	25%
45–54	85%	15%
55–64	86%	14%
65–74	87%	13%
75 or Older	82%	18%
By Sleep Pattern		
Early Riser	86%	14%
Night Owl	80%	20%
By Outlook		
Optimist	87%	13%
Pessimist	72%	28%

READY TO TAKE CONTROL OF YOUR MONEY?

Take our FREE 3-minute assessment to find out where you need to start.

We'll show you how to dump debt, save for emergencies, and build wealth. We'll give you a free, customized financial plan, along with free tools and resources. It's all about getting on the right financial plan. You can make a change! We'll help you.

For more information, visit

WWW.RAMSEYSOLUTIONS.COM/STARTNOW

You CAN baby step your way to being a *millionaire*.

Did you know 33% of millionaires never had a six-figure household income? That means no matter your current situation or background, when you follow a proven plan, you can build wealth! These folks are doing it—and you can too!

Yesenia & Luis
are living free and building their future!

WE'RE DEBT FREE! $60,000 IN 5 YEARS

WE PAID OFF THE HOUSE! #DEBTFREE

Scott & Rachel
paid off their house!

Maddi & John
are Baby Steps Millionaires!